Golden Angels

A Pet Loss Memoir

by Stephanie Weaver

To Cheryl—

In honor of your angels—

In peace + healing—

Stephan Wen

Golden Angels

For Pete Andrews, one of Buddy's dearest friends.
You left us far too soon.

Golden Angels: A Pet Loss Memoir
Copyright © 2013 by Stephanie Weaver

Editor: Maraya Cornell
Copy Editors: Marjorie Schwarzer, Elizabeth Perhac Schmitt, and Susan Cesen
Book Design: Tanya Bredehoft of Artefact Design
Photography: Stephanie Weaver

For further information contact:

Braver Endeavor Press
P.O. Box 35054
San Diego, CA 92163
www.braverendeavor.com

Printed in the United States by Braver Endeavor Press

ISBN-13: 978-0-9888619-9-2
ISBN-10: 0988861992

Table of Contents

Foreword

Buddy Girl   Daisy May

Grieving is exhausting. I began writing this book as a tribute to our beloved Golden retriever Buddy Girl, who we lost to cancer on January 2, 2012. Since then we have lost seven human family members, so the process of grieving has been part of my life all year.

Everyone grieves differently. In my case, I immediately started writing about Buddy Girl, using my creativity as a way to process my grief and hold on to her memory. A few of the essays became blog posts, and then this book began to take shape. I hope these thirteen essays—and the healthy recipes that accompany them—help you savor your loved ones and those you have lost, whether they had four legs or two.

My husband Bob and I have been blessed to have two incredible dogs in our family. Buddy Girl was our first dog: graceful, beautiful, spirited. We found our little Daisy on Mother's Day 2012. While she can't replace Buddy Girl, she has brought new joy, challenges, and healing to our lives.

• • •

January 2, 2012: Bob and I woke up late that day and neither of us wanted to get up. Buddy Girl was sleeping with her head shoved under the bed, our Headless Puppy. I knew it was the last time I would wake up with her there. It was hard for me to breathe.

Bob said, "This is Buddy's day. It's a celebration of her. We have to focus on the joy." We lit a candle and I laid out the pack of angel cards face down on the table. Angel cards come in a small fabric bag covered in hearts. Each card has a single word on it like *Love*, *Acceptance*, or *Balance* with a sweet watercolor illustration. They can be used for fun, for guidance, for meditation. Some people pick one every day, others once a week. Bob and I pick them together on special occasions, especially when we are starting something new. A new year, a new phase.

We spent some time meditating, setting our intention for the day. We wanted the day to be beautiful, to enjoy it, to stay present.

I picked *Creativity*. Hmm. Not even close to what I was expecting. Bob picked Release. Okay, that made sense. We each picked a second card. I picked *Obedience*. Hunh? I tried not to be annoyed, knowing that it would make sense at some point. Bob's last card was *Patience*. We used the angel cards as a way to frame the day. The cards we chose became more meaningful as the weeks passed.

I've named each essay here after an angel card. It may sound a little sappy but Bob and I frequently called Buddy our guardian angel, and I wonder how we would have gotten through some very tough times without her.

Daisy appeared in our lives just when we needed her, keeping us company during the loss of our dear friend Pete in June and our nephew in August. It's truly not an exaggeration to say that these special dogs have acted as angels in our lives, bringing healing and joy, keeping us grounded and present, and helping us experience the infinite power of love. This is their story, and with all stories, we must begin.

Begin

HER INDEPENDENCE, RESPONSIVENESS, & SPIRIT IMPRESSED US

The ear kiss clinched it!

Here's Buddy! 6 weeks.

Begin

Buddy's story started long before she was born, or I met Bob. I had wanted a dog for the entire 15 years I lived in Chicago. But I was always in an apartment, always at work or with friends. There was never space nor time enough to care properly for a dog.

When I moved to San Diego to work for the San Diego Zoo, getting a dog was a top priority. I had downsized from a ten-room apartment in Chicago to two small rooms on the second floor of a building with a slow elevator. I had a twelve-square patch of kitchenette linoleum and wall-to-wall shag carpeting. But I was determined to get my dog at last.

There it was, the posting on the Zoo bulletin board. Free puppies! I called to reserve one, made an appointment for Saturday, and went off to the pet store, where I dropped $90 on everything I'd need for my new Buddy. I had no idea how popular that name was. I just knew I needed a Buddy. So I bought the little custom engraved nametag and counted the days until I could pick up my puppy.

On Saturday, I called for directions to the property out in Jamul. "Oh, I'm sorry. All the puppies are gone."

"Wha---?" But I have a crate! And Baby Dog shampoo! And a cute little leash and collar!

And a friggin' engraved nametag with my address on it!

I was totally crushed even though I realized that trying to housebreak a puppy in that tiny apartment without access to a yard would have been a disaster. I could have gotten a dog someplace else, but the reality of the limitations of that apartment had settled in and I knew I needed to wait a little longer.

Six months later I started dating Bob. Six months after that, we bought our house. It has a fenced-in yard. Commence puppy planning.

Not so fast. Bob wanted time to work on the property and enjoy being married before taking on the responsibility of a dog. He knew that it wasn't fair to get a dog while working on the house, and our house needed a lot of work.

I had been hinting that I wanted a dog for a while when Christmas came around. Bob is an excellent stuffer of Christmas stockings, and he really outdid himself that first Christmas. Amidst all the fun little gifts, he tucked in a Golden Retriever puppy refrigerator magnet.

A year went by, we worked on the house, and I kept hinting. In my second Christmas stocking I got a little stuffed Golden Retriever. Bob says now that he wasn't trying to taunt me; he just thought it was cute.

Our third Christmas I got Buddy Girl, and she got her own stocking.

All along, I had thought we would go to a nice shelter and pick out a dog. Since I worked at a zoo I knew all about inbreeding, puppy mills, and the importance of rescuing shelter animals. In that world, people didn't buy purebreds, they Rescued.

After two-and-a-half years of cajoling, I didn't even think about asking for a puppy. But now that he was ready, he was Ready, all in. In his mind, the process went like this...

"Let's do some research on breeds, and figure out what breed we think will really suit us. And of course, don't you want a puppy so you can train it from the start?" Do I want a puppy?! Are you kidding? So on a sunny Sunday afternoon in October 2000 we went to the bookstore for an afternoon of puppy research.

Golden Retrievers weren't on my radar, but let's not forget about the magnet and the stuffed animal. A seed had been sown. We kept coming back to Goldens: how smart they were, how easily trained, how much they loved people. We both liked bigger dogs, but Goldens weren't TOO big. Well, they weren't mastiffs or Great Danes, right?

After paging through a pile of books we bought a small one about the breed. On the third page is a hilarious picture of a woman in a black outfit with a Golden puppy. She is covered in fur. The caption reads, "If you prefer to dress in dark colors, the Golden Retriever can be an exasperating living companion." And we laughed and said, "Oh, it can't really be that bad!"

Hah.

The next week we started looking in the Want Ads; two litters of Goldens were for sale. We made appointments. Both litters would be old enough to go home for Christmas. Perfect!

The first litter turned out to be a backyard-breeder-puppy-mill situation. What tipped us off? The female had been bred too young; they had no AKC papers or health certifications; the pups were inconsistent in looks and temperament; and the sellers were totally focused on the price, not whether we would give their dog a good home.

We headed out to the other place. It was a long drive, with a stop at KFC for biscuits and cole slaw. The breeders owned an avocado ranch, and their dogs were in a concrete kennel. Now if I hadn't been working at a zoo at the time, the concrete kennel might have put me off. But I understood that they were serious dog breeders, and this was a really, really nice kennel. Well built. Super clean and well maintained. We met the mom, Molly, and she was a sweetheart. A perfectly sized 60-pound female. They showed us the photo of the male, a striking, glossy show dog. This was a good start.

The breeders took us to the whelping box, which was glowing and toasty under the heat lamp. They opened the lid, and we saw the litter.

Nine warm, snuggly puppies, every one the same precise shade of whipped honey. The first word that popped into my head was: *Quality*.

Here's what the experts tell you about picking out puppies. You aren't supposed to get attached to any of them on the first visit. Pick them all up, interact with them, and see who responds to you. Watch their energy, don't take the runt of the litter...

So what did I do? I picked up one of the girls, who promptly fell asleep in the crook of my arm. And I held her for forty-five minutes while the breeders grilled us about our fitness as prospective puppy parents.

What kind of yard did we have? What was the fence like? How many hours did we work? Where was the dog going to sleep? What were we planning on feeding it?

The breeders made us page through the *Big Book of Goldens* to see pictures of all the litters' forebears. Big, gorgeous dogs with American Kennel Club names like *Sonny's Morning Gold-Rush* and *Sunkota's Electrick*. We had no interest in showing or breeding, but these professional breeders were so proud of their dogs that we dutifully feigned interest until they would let us write a deposit check. After an hour of grilling and ill-advised puppy snuggling, we finally got them to take our money. We would come back in two weeks to pick out our puppy.

Little did we know that she had already picked us.

Beyond excited, we drove back out to the avocado ranch on a sunny Saturday afternoon. We had responded to the ad early enough to have the first pick of the litter, after they chose one for a companion animal program. We had already decided we wanted a girl, which left us with six puppies to choose from.

Five of the girls were sleepy and completely uninterested in us. One was totally awake. I am convinced to this day that it was Buddy I held for that first 45 minutes, imprinting my scent on her. She chased the ball, she chased us, we picked her up, she kissed and nibbled our ears with her needle-like puppy teeth. At one point, Bob stepped behind a short fence. She ran to the fence, got up on her squatty little hind legs, put her front paws on the fence, and went, "Wham, wham, wham, wham, wham!" trying to get at him. We said, "Oh my gosh, how cute is that?"

You know what? Not so cute at two AM when the pen is next to your bed.

They say your dog picks you. And we surely needed her, although we had no idea how much, or what she was destined to teach us.

At seven-and-a-half weeks, Buddy came home on December 23rd, 2000. Our adventure was just beginning.

Grapefruit-avocado-kumquat salad—*for people*

This fresh and delicious salad always reminds me of the avocado farm where we met Buddy Girl.

Serves 4

2 Blanco D'Oro grapefruit
2 ripe avocados
3–4 kumquats
1 T. (*15 ml*) agave syrup or honey
1 T. (*15 ml*) cassis [black currant] vinegar
1 handful fresh mint leaves

You are going to *macerate* the grapefruit and kumquats for several hours or overnight before serving this. Macerating is a technique where fruit is combined with some kind of sugar, which creates a syrup as it draws liquid out of the fruit. In the case of grapefruit and kumquats, it sweetens them enough to balance the flavors.

Whisk the agave syrup or honey together with the vinegar in a bowl large enough to hold the salad.

Start by cutting off each end of the grapefruit, then slicing off all the peel, using a serrated knife. You should always use a serrated knife on citrus peel, as cutting it can dull regular knives. You should now have a naked grapefruit with very little white pith left.

Switching to a sharp paring knife, cut each individual section of grapefruit into the bowl with the syrup-vinegar mixture, leaving the pith between each segment behind. When you have cut all the segments into the bowl, squeeze all the juice out of what remains in your hand. You have made "supremes." Not to be confused with the Motown group.

Slice the kumquats as thinly as possible and add them to the bowl. Remove any seeds.

Toss the fruit with the syrup, then cover and refrigerate for several hours or overnight.

Just before serving, cut each avocado in half lengthwise, then twist the halves apart. Using a sharp paring knife, score the avocado in both directions (cutting just to the peel but not through it), then use a grapefruit spoon to scoop out the square sections into the bowl with the grapefruit.

Finely chop the mint and add to the bowl. Toss. Add a small amount of salt if you like.

Notes: You can use any type of grapefruit if you can't find Blanco d'Oro. If you can't find black currant vinegar, any fruity vinegar, like balsamic or pomegranate, will work. If kumquats are not in season you can use mandarin oranges or clementines. **Avocados are people-food only.**

Parenthood

Parenthood

One year when I was in my twenties, I attended twelve weddings, eight baby showers, and six housewarming parties. It felt like everyone I knew had great things happening in their lives. My life was an endless stream of gift registries, cards, and presents celebrating other people's happiness.

When people at these events would inevitably ask me if I wanted kids I would always answer: "If I get married and if he wants kids and if he will totally help, then yes I'd consider adoption."

Don't get me wrong. I really like kids. Having seen so many friends and family members become parents, I have an idea of the joys and sacrifices, and I don't think you should do it unless you can wholeheartedly give what's required. I've always enjoyed my nieces and nephews and our neighbors' kids. More than twenty kids live on my block right now, and most are under the age of 13.

Once I met Mr. Right-For-Me and got married, I was 38 and he was 40. We'd waited a long time to find each other, and we wanted to enjoy being married. About the time we needed to make the final decision whether to have kids, I became really sick and it was several years before I was truly well. At that point, the window was closed. Occasionally we talk about how it would have

been cool to see what our baby would have been like, but we are content with our path.

I never thought that getting a dog would be a substitute for having a kid, and honestly, people who treated their dogs like children creeped me out. I knew that a dog is an animal that needs to be trained. I had no intention of having my new dog sleep in our bed, eat our food, or be obnoxiously ill-behaved. I was a big fan of the television show The Dog Whisperer.

And then we picked out Buddy, or she picked us, and something in me started to melt. We had had her about a week and were doing our best to follow all the rules in the books. The pack leader has to have the top position, and physically be highest, so no bed, no couch, no lap for the puppy. But oh my word, she was so insanely cute! So to follow the rules, we would watch TV sitting on the floor in the back room with her between us.

One night, I looked down at my little fluffball. She was sacked out with her head towards me, her front paws stretched out, her little back legs delicately crossed. And a wave of love engulfed me. My eyes filled with tears. I looked at Bob, who looked alarmed. Why was his wife suddenly crying?

• • •

I LOVE her!

Um, honey? What's wrong?

I LOVE her!

Uh, okay.

I could never explain it. But from that second on, I was her mom. I honestly cannot imagine loving a human child more than I loved that dog. I'm sure it's got to be different, more somehow, but I cannot fathom how. What floored me about growing to love Buddy Girl, and now Daisy, is how our capacity to love just exponentially increases when we open our hearts. Even when someone is gone, we can love them just as much as we did when they were alive, even though they're not here breathing. Death doesn't kill love.

. . .

I loved Buddy's little feet and her silky ears that got wavy when wet. I loved her soft little puppy tummy. I loved the way her tail was so expressive, so fully articulated. She could wave just the tip of it, or undulate the entire length of it. I loved her beautiful golden feathers when they grew in. And I loved her face and her smile.

I loved how her lip would get caught in one of her canines, and we'd call her Snaggletooth. I loved how she completely manipulated Bob into feeding her cookies.

I loved giving her puzzles to solve and watching her mind work. She could get the lid off an empty bottle in about five seconds, turn the bottle upside down, work the kibble or cookies out of it and then come back for a refill.

I loved how she would toddle off to bed when she was tired, and how she learned to ask to go outside when she had to pee and ring the bell to come in. I loved how she would lie on the floor on my side of the bed and I could slide my foot out from under the covers and pet her. I loved waking up in the morning to see her splayed out on her back, her paws up over her head and her back legs akimbo in the most unladylike of positions.

I loved the way she played with her toys. She'd take a ball and lie on her back, holding it up near her mouth and spinning it around with her paws. She'd rip the hard plastic eyes off each and every toy we bought her, and then play with them for years, never tearing them again. She would pick up three foam balls in her mouth at a time and carry them around the house.

And then there was Fluffy (or Cinnamon, or Sandy) the enormous toy du Noel. Every year I would buy her a gigantic stuffed toy for Christmas, usually a bear. She would carry it around by the neck, dominate it with some more unladylike behavior, then lie down with her mouth clamped down on its neck, always its neck, and spend at least 30 minutes suffocating it.

. . .

Even when she drove me crazy with her barking, I loved her. And I did all the things a mother would do. I made sure she ate properly. I set up play dates with other puppies and made sure she exercised. I took her to the vet. I brushed out her tangles. I put medicine on her irritated skin and in her itchy ears. I trimmed her paws and clipped her nails. Bob would always say, "She loves it when you take care of her. You're her momma."

I am incredibly blessed in my husband and am grateful every day that we found each other. It may have taken me a while to convince Bob to get a dog, or as he would say, a while for him to be ready, but once he committed, that was it.

. . .

Bob approached puppy fatherhood far differently than I approached puppy motherhood. I focused on discipline; Bob was all about fun. After his thoughtful analysis of breeds, ages, and litters, he simply fell in love. It took a while for him to admit it, but Buddy started melting Bob's heart the day we picked her out.

He was the one who hated trying to crate train her. He was the one who played and napped with her on the floor. It was Bob who made her toys come to life. It was him who brought her home a new toy after every single business trip, and rolled up his dirty socks for her to carry around as he unpacked.

It was Bob who borrowed a video camera from work and made the elaborate, toy-centric puppy videos that still charm me. While photos of our Puppy Love are very good, video is even better.

It was Bob who wanted to make Buddy's dinners more interesting, feeling that kibble was not enough for her. He stocked the cookies and the peanut butter to stuff her Kong toy.

Bob's relationship with his girl was totally different than mine. I was always thinking about discipline. Were we being too easy on her? Why wasn't she heeling properly? Was she getting another ear infection? Was she chewing her paw again? Should we take another obedience class? Was her diet healthy enough?

Bob's walks with Bud were long, easy rambles, full of sniffing and pinecones and cookies. My walks involved a pedometer, brisk pace, and frequent power struggles every time she tried to stop and sniff. It was me who wielded the nail clippers and trimmers, and Bob who bribed her with cookies to stay still.

I would buy her one big toy for Christmas. He bought her five, plus a whole stocking. I loved watching him do it because he got so much pleasure out of it. He would wrap them in newspaper or plain heavy tissue, once he learned that she could unwrap them herself.

So many times, when we'd be talking about a weekend getaway, or going out for dinner or a concert in the park, he'd say, "Can Buddy come?" And we'd bring her, even though she did not do well in those situations. There was a lot of whining and begging and leash-pulling. And I might have left her home, but she was his girl.

During the last four years of Bud's life, Bob was away during the week. So weekends were precious for all of us. Once Bob arrived around 10 pm on Friday, Bud would climb up on him on the recliner. Two paws up, two down was the rule. Sometimes a third paw would creep up off the carpet, just to test the waters. She might have a ball, or be after his dinner or his bowl of tortilla chips, or just want to lick him all over. But they would have Poppa time together.

I enjoyed how sweet he was with her. She softened him over the years; the heart-melting that had begun on the very first day never stopped. We had some rough work-related times over the years we had Bud, and through all of our challenges she was a constant. Always there. Always love. Always his girl.

. . .

We had meant to bathe her the week before her last Christmas, but she had seemed very tired and we were busy with the holidays. She was overdue for a paw trimming as well. Goldens get crazy hairy paws, with hair growing out from between their toes every which way. Despite her having a weird cough that started Christmas week, we didn't know how sick she was. Once we found out that she had advanced cancer, we weren't going to tire her out by giving her a bath. But her paws really bugged me. I wanted to send her to heaven clean, or at least with a pedicure.

She never liked having her paws trimmed. It was a two-person job, Bob with the cookies to bribe her into submission, and me with the clippers. On her last morning, I woke up and she was in her bed. I knelt down and kissed her and petted her for a while. She looked exhausted. I realized I could probably trim her paws if I did it right there. So I got the clippers and a towel to catch the hair and started trimming. I knew she was feeling poorly because she lay there calmly, allowing me to groom her one last time. I gave her pretty lion paws for her last day. I knew it was unimportant, silly even, but it felt like the right thing to do. She was such a beauty, and I wanted her to look her best.

When I picked up her remains from the vet, I found a final paw print in clay in the bag. It made me satisfied, even in my grief, because her paw was so pretty, so tidy.

Peanut butter kiss cookies—*for people*

Bob and Buddy Girl both loved peanut butter. BG would get it in her Kong; Bob eats it whenever possible. Buddy loved giving kisses, too.

Makes 2 dozen

1 C. (*110 g*) sifted gluten-free flour mix
1/2 t. (*1 g*) baking soda
1/2 t. (*1 g*) baking powder
1/2 t. (*1 g*) salt
1/4 C. (*60 g*) vegan margarine
1/4 C. (*60 g*) natural peanut butter or sunflower seed butter
1/2 C. (*80 g*) granulated maple, coconut, or organic cane sugar
1 t. (*5 ml*) vanilla
1 T. (*5 g*) flaxseed meal plus 2 T. (*30 ml*) filtered water—or 1 egg
24 semi-sweet fair trade chocolate morsels or peanut butter cups

Preheat oven to 375F/*170C/gas mark 5*. Line baking sheets with parchment paper.

Sift together flour, baking powder and soda, and salt.

Put the flaxseed meal in a deep mixing bowl (or stand mixer bowl) with the water. Let stand five minutes. Cream the margarine, nut butter, sugar, and vanilla together with the flax meal.

Add the flour mixture; mix well. Chill in the freezer for 30–45 minutes until very firm.

Take a level tablespoon of dough and roll between your palms into a round ball. Roll lightly in more of your granulated sugar. Place on the prepared cookie sheets, then flatten with your hand. Bake in preheated oven 8 minutes, rotating the pans at 4 minutes so the cookies bake evenly.

While the cookies are baking, unwrap your chocolates.

Pull out the warm cookies and press one chocolate into the center of each cookie. Return to the oven and bake 3–4 minutes more.

Cool on wire racks. Store in metal cookie tins for best results.

Notes: I used half gluten-free oat flour and half Bob's Red Mill all-purpose baking mix, a blend that includes bean flours. If you can eat peanuts, use peanut butter for the most authentic flavor, but sunflower seed butter also tastes great.
[We eventually switched over to sunflower seed butter, as it seemed to reduce her ear infections.] Use whatever kind of organic granulated sugar product works best for you: maple sugar, low-glycemic coconut sugar, cane sugar, palm sugar, or Florida crystals. These cookies are vegan if you use vegan chocolates.

Patience

Patience

When we first picked the *Patience* angel card on Buddy's last day in January 2012, I assumed it simply meant waiting. Waiting to heal, waiting for the right puppy, waiting for the grief to ease. And it was. I really needed to wait.

I have always been a champ at delayed gratification. When I was a kid, I would save the very best candy bar from Halloween for last. I would put that full-sized Snickers bar in the back of the top shelf in my closet, eating the Smarties, then the Tootsie Rolls, then the Sugar Babies, working my way up the sugar hierarchy through that pillowcase of loot. Sometimes the good candy bar would actually be stale by the time I got to it.

When it comes to money and planning, I'm a patient person. I'll painstakingly save the money for an expensive purchase or a trip. The planning and anticipation are part of the fun for me.

With grieving, not so much. I have a journal entry dated mid-January that declares: *I want to go buy a puppy TODAY.*

I quickly grew tired of crying in yoga class. The house felt way too empty, too quiet, and every day I wanted to go out and get a dog. I nearly rescued one that showed up lost at the neighborhood dog wash, just so I could have someone in the house. I sought any excuse to get out of the house every day. It felt that quiet and that... wrong.

Grieving was so variable. One day I would be fine all the way through my yoga class and think, "There, I'm getting better." Two days later, I would cry throughout the entire class, feeling as raw and desolate as the day Buddy died. I felt like I was back at square one and had made no progress at all.

After a few weeks of grieving for Buddy, I stopped waking up thinking she would be in her bed next to me, and I finally stopped imagining that I heard her shake her dog tags when I opened the front door. But still I missed her like crazy every minute of every day. While I wished it didn't hurt so much, I also didn't want to forget her.

I thought that it would be easier once a new dog arrived, filling up the space, keeping me busy. But I didn't want to forget how special Buddy Girl was. I wanted to be farther along in the grieving process, farther away from the pain of my loss, but each day that went by was a day farther away from her being alive, and that made me sad.

What I learned is that there aren't any shortcuts to the grieving process. You know you need to keep living your life, and your lost loved one wouldn't want you to keep your life on hold, yet it feels like you are loving them less if you do start to fall in love with someone else.

I totally understand why people go straight out and get a new dog after they have lost one. But there aren't any shortcuts to doing the work of grieving a loss. You can get a new dog, but you still have to grieve for the one you lost.

. . .

As soon as we picked Daisy up, I realized there was another dimension to the *Patience* card.

Now it's about p-a-t-i-e-n-c-e. Puppies don't know anything except how to wrestle, bite, eat, sleep, and poop. They don't know how to wear a collar. They don't know how to walk on a lead. They don't know that they're supposed to go outside to pee. They don't know what *sit*, *down*, or *stay* means. They don't know anything.

And teaching them everything takes patience.

I didn't realize how much we had taught Buddy Girl until Daisy came along. Buddy had learned well over 150 words; Bob counted one time, in an effort to privately compete with a border collie that made the news. We could communicate with Buddy in that easy shorthand of family.

Daisy is lovely: bright, funny, sweet, cute as a button. She reminds me of Buddy, and I often call her Buddy by mistake. I felt my heart

wanting to give in to Daisy, wanting to melt, and yet I also held back for a while. Maybe if I didn't fall in love as much, it wouldn't hurt as much at the end. And I knew that a few months wasn't enough time to grieve a love like I had for Buddy Girl.

As the weeks with Daisy went on—partly because I was exhausted from getting up in the middle of the night—I found myself getting blue. Daisy was fun but frustrating, and some days I just ached for Buddy to come back. Bud liked to be right nearby as I worked; Daisy could spend all day in the yard without us if we let her. Bud was a cuddly puppy; Daisy was a biter.

The biting. Oh the biting. I am sure that Buddy did a little bit of biting, but teaching her to ease up and have a soft mouth went pretty quickly. Daisy was all shark teeth and she was pouncy. I would be talking on iChat, letting my guard down for a moment, and she would come flying through the air to chomp on my arm. Or she would fling herself at my pants and rip through my jeans when I thought she was across the yard. We would be having a nice little round of fetch, and then suddenly—whammo!—my arm was bleeding again.

She was my living meditation lesson: a daily, hourly, minutely reminder to breathe, relax, try again. Try again. Try again.

I couldn't expect Daisy at three months old to heel or even to stop biting. I couldn't expect her to be Buddy Girl. But I could be patient. I could be aware. I could let go of expectation, be present, and recognize how fast her puppyhood was speeding by. At six months the biting was a distant memory, the scars on my arm just faintly pink. Daisy became more and more fun as the weeks passed, and my patience was rewarded. All too soon she'll be a big dog and I'll be nostalgic when I look at her videos.

· · ·

There are glimmers of what our future holds, Daisy and I. I learned to cuddle her right when she woke up; she makes this little contentment noise that's completely endearing. I'm still working hard training her to heel, and walks are so much more pleasant than they were with a big puller like Bud who wanted to stop and sniff every five feet. She is no longer wild, nor under house arrest in the kitchen, and she gets cuddlier and more mellow every day.

My grief eased over time and Daisy holds a different place in my heart. I'm glad we waited five months after Buddy died to get another dog so that Daisy had a better chance of being loved for her own unique qualities, instead of as a replacement for someone else.

Slow-cooked beans with extra thyme—*for people*

For an essay on patience, it seemed appropriate to share my method of cooking dried beans, which require an overnight soak but are totally worth it. This method, which I refer to as Beany-Brothy Deliciousness, yields delicious vegetable stock, plus cooked veggies that blend up into a tasty pureed soup or can be served as a veggie mash. Patience offers many rewards.

Makes 5 cups of cooked beans, plus tons of broth, and two servings of pureed soup

2 C. (1 lb./*450 g*) dried beans
3 carrots, *any size*
4 stalks celery
1 onion, white, yellow, or brown onion, *any size*
2 cloves garlic
2 red potatoes, optional
fennel tops (3–5 fronds)
thyme sprigs (handful or a package)
2 bay leaves
2 T. (*10 g*) kosher salt
6 T. (*90 ml*) olive oil
8 C. (*2 L*) filtered water

Pour out the dry beans into a shallow bowl, a bit at a time, and pick through them. Remove any pebbles, sticks, or discolored beans. Some people remove broken beans. I'm not that picky. But I've found pebbles before so don't skip this step.

Put the sorted beans in a large pot and rinse and swirl with enough water to cover them. I use tap water for this step. Drain completely.

Cover the beans with enough *filtered* water to allow them to double in size. Leave on the counter overnight.

In the morning, rinse and drain the beans.

Return them to the cooking pot. Prep the vegetables and add them to the pot as you go:

Scrub the carrots and celery, cut off the tops and bottoms, and cut into three large chunks.

Cut off the stem end of the onion. Then cut it in half lengthwise through the root end. Peel off the papery skin. If you want onions in with your beans at the end, slice the onion lengthwise. If you want the beans to go off and have another beany life in a different recipe, quarter the onion, leaving it attached at the root end so you can easily remove it.

Smash the garlic cloves under the flat blade of your chef's knife. Kapow! Remove the papery skin.

Scrub the potatoes, peel if desired, and cut into large chunks or small dice. (If you want potato dice in your beans at the end, dice the potatoes. If you want to be able to fish the pieces out, cut into quarters.)

Tie the washed fennel fronds and thyme sprigs into a bundle with some clean kitchen twine.

Add the bay leaves, salt, olive oil, and filtered water.

Bring just to a boil with the lid on the pot, then turn down to a simmer (just barely bubbling). Check the beans after 30 minutes. You want them to be nicely tender but not falling apart.

Depending on the size, age, and type of beans and how much they soften from soaking, they cook in 30–120 minutes.

Once the beans are done, remove the herb bundle and bay leaves and compost them. Fish out the large chunks of veggies with a slotted spoon. You can mash those up or blend them with some of the Brothy Deliciousness (BD) to make a lovely veggie soup. Drain the extra BD into a container. Use it to make gravy or in place of water to cook rice, quinoa, or millet.

Serve the drained beans as is, or use them in any recipe calling for cooked beans.

Notes: You can use this method to cook any type of dried beans. Lentils and split peas will cook very quickly, possibly in as little as 20 minutes. Larger, tougher beans might take 2 hours of cooking, so be patient and taste them every 15 minutes until they're tender but not mushy. Freeze in one cup portions to use instead of canned beans.

Love

Love

The day you bring home a dog, the clock starts. You know, without a shadow of a doubt, that you will bury that dog. And the more you love that dog, the worse their death is going to hurt.

You know it, yet you bring home the dog. Because having the dog and loving the dog are worth every second of pain when you lose them.

The first few years with Buddy, this happy little thought would cross my mind: "It is going to be devastating when she dies." I often said to her, "You are going to have to give us 15 years, okay?" And she would look at me and love me back.

I would push the thought away and try my best to stay in the present. I fed her the best food we could afford, kept her away from chemicals, cooked organic veggies for her. All in the hopes of keeping her as healthy as possible, so she could stay with us a long time.

I like to listen to CDs by a teacher named Esther Hicks. On one CD, a person asks about beloved pets, stating that one pet he had as a child seemed very similar to a dog he had later. Esther replies that beloved pets return to us many times over our lifetimes, although they might not look the same. That might seem crazy to you, but this idea has always given me enormous comfort.

When the thought of Buddy's death would pop into my head, I would look at Buddy and whisper to her, "You're coming back, right? You know you have to come back?" And she would look at me and love me, and sometimes I imagined that I heard her say "Yes."

. . .

When you know the pure unadulterated love of a dog like Buddy Girl, you are changed forever. It's truly not an exaggeration to say that everyone loved Buddy. Total strangers would stop their cars in the middle of the road to see her when she was a puppy, and people would cross the street in order to pet her.

She had all of her favorite stops in the neighborhood... she got big cookies at our neighborhood market, and little cookies at the high school, and cookies delivered by a lady named Gail. Everywhere Buddy went, people loved her.

Older men who walked by themselves, heads down, lost in their sadness or illness slowly warmed up to her. I imagined her lovely spirit broke through their fog and helped thaw them a bit. Eventually I learned their names, and their faces would lighten a little as they stopped to pet her.

More than half of our friends are Buddy connections. We met all the neighbors on our block and dog owners at the park, and an entire social circle developed. Her doggie friends became our friends, we learned their owners' names, and eventually started socializing with them outside the park. We went to baby showers and barbecues and weddings. We saw their kids arrive and turn one and two and six.

They were the people who came on her last weekend to say goodbye. Some had cared for her when I was traveling, and loved her as much as their own sweet dogs. One confessed that she was more attached to Bud than she was to her own dog. These are the people who cried with us when they learned that she was gone.

Many of us spend our lives trying to find that kind of love. We seek it in others. We seek to define it as God, Allah, Christ, Buddha, or some other name. I grew up Christian, and there is a lot in Christian doctrine about unconditional love. That God loves us no matter what, despite our flaws, in all circumstances. We work so hard to try to connect to God, to understand God, to feel His or Her presence.

All we need to do is look into those liquid, brown, loving eyes. That's God. Because it's pure love. You don't have to repent. You don't even have to say you're sorry for anything. It's there every day. Every time you wake up. Every time you come home. There is never a bad day. No complaints. Always so happy to see you. Your coming home is the best thing that ever happened to her. Every time. Every day. Every morning. If that isn't God, what is?

And so, when that love passes on, it leaves a profound mark. The deeper the love, the deeper the mark. While we will always have a Buddy-shaped space in our lives, I wouldn't trade one second of that love.

. . .

What still amazes me is that we have a seemingly infinite capacity to love, our hearts continue to expand, and new people and animals can step into our hearts. Every day I love Daisy a little bit more, yet that love doesn't diminish one bit of what I felt for Buddy Girl. And that's a wonderful thing.

Birthday cake—*for dogs only*

Love takes many forms, and when you have a kid, sometimes it takes the form of a birthday party.

Buddy's second birthday fell on a weekend. Six dogs came with their humans. It was hilarious to watch them playing together. While we had some snacks, the biggest hit of the party was Buddy's cake. It allowed me to be a mom, making something cute for my kid.

The dogs gobbled it down, and then went off for another round of playtime.

Notes: If you bring doggy birthday cake to a dog park, you run the risk of creating a small riot. Always give treats to the owner, not the dog.

Serves up to 12 dogs, although that's not recommended in a small back yard!

For the cake you'll need:
Cornbread (recipe follows)
Liverwurst (about 4 oz/120 g)
Kitchen Bouquet (liquid caramel food coloring)
Cheez Whiz or other canned cheez
Rawhide "sticks" for candles, *optional*

Cornbread

Makes one pan. Feel free to cut off a hunk for yourself before "frosting" it for the dogs.

1 C. (*250 ml*) soymilk or lowfat milk
1 T. (*15 ml*) apple cider vinegar
1 T. (*5 g*) ground flax seeds (or 1 egg) plus
 2 T. (*30 ml*) filtered water (omit if using egg)
1/4 C. (*60 ml*) filtered water
2 T. (*30 ml*) olive oil
1 C. (*170 g*) yellow corn meal
1 C. (*125 g*) gluten-free flour mix or regular wheat flour
2 t. (*4 g*) baking powder
1/2 t. (*1 g*) baking soda

Preheat the oven to 400F/*180C/gas mark 6*. Put a cast iron skillet in the oven to preheat. (You can also use an 8" round or square pan. Line the pan with parchment paper and oil it with cooking spray. Do not preheat.)

Add the vinegar to the soy or lowfat milk, stir, and let stand to curdle.

Whisk together the corn meal, flour, baking powder, and baking soda in a medium bowl.

Put the flax seeds and water in your mixing bowl and let stand to thicken. (If using an egg, add it in at the next step.)

With a wooden spoon (or a stand mixer), mix together the curdled soymilk, flax seed mixture or egg, water, and olive oil until blended. Add the flour mixture and mix just until incorporated. Do not overmix.

Remove the skillet from the oven with a hot pad. Put about 1 T. (*15 ml*) of oil in the skillet and tilt to cover the bottom and sides of the pan evenly.

Pour the batter into the pan and spread evenly. Place in the center of the oven and bake for 15–20 minutes. Remove, cool, and decorate as described.

Frosting

Cut up the liverwurst into chunks and put into a saucepan with about 1 T. (*15 ml*) Kitchen Bouquet. Melt over low-medium heat and whisk until the liverwurst has become a smooth consistency. Add enough Kitchen Bouquet so it looks like chocolate frosting. You can also simply blend the liverwurst and the Kitchen Bouquet in a food processor until it's smooth, creamy, and the proper "chocolate" color.

Immediately spread over the cooled yellow cake.

Use the canned cheez to write on the cake and create swirls or flowers. If you want candles, place the rawhide sticks into the cake, topping them with canned cheez flames.

Make sure all the dogs at the party can eat all the ingredients before serving. Cut into smallish pieces and place on paper plates. Have each owner take their dog and its plate to a separate area. Feed them all at the same time. You can always send extra cake home with the dogs for the next day.

Make sure you don't give the rawhide candles to any dogs that might choke on them or who have trouble digesting rawhide.

Obedience

Obedience

One of the angel cards I drew on Buddy's last day was *Obedience*. And my first thought was annoyance. "What kind of a weird, crappy angel card is that? Bob picks *Release* and I pick *Obedience*?"

But, having chosen angel cards for many years, I know that I always pick the cards I need at the time. If one doesn't make sense or feels hard to understand, it usually proves to be the best teacher in the end.

I started thinking about the word *Obedience* that first week after she passed. First, there was the obvious dog-obedience connection. I knew that when we did get our new puppy, the whole next year would be about obedience training.

Second, my friend Marjorie said that a key element of obedience is trust. You have to earn your dog's trust in order for them to obey you; it's not an automatic thing. If you trust an authority, whether it's an institution or someone in power, you can obey them. If you trust that something is good for you, you will obey it. People who follow an organized religion trust both the tenets of that religion and its leaders, which allows them to obey and follow those teachings. I did trust that eventually we would be okay, and that another wonderful dog would come into our lives.

Third, a synonym for obedience is discipline. And that sent my mind in an interesting direction. Where is the discipline in grieving?

I see it as the difference between grieving and wallowing.

. . .

Grieving is picking up the shopping list you made the week before she died and seeing tuna written on it. You are hit with the loss again. You were going to buy her tuna because she wasn't feeling well and you hoped to tempt her with something special. But you never got to the store because you found out she had cancer and she probably wouldn't have eaten the tuna anyway and then she was gone. It's okay to stand there and sob for a while with the shopping list in your hand, holding the counter so you don't fall over.

Wallowing is saying, "I'll never buy her tuna again, or cookies, or make her dinner, or take her for walks..." and continuing on in that direction. Thinking that way doesn't honor her. It's living in the past. It's creating more misery in yourself than needs to be there. It's about feeling sorry for yourself instead of honoring the loss.

That's how I interpret discipline. It reminds me of the most challenging phrase from Buddhist teachings: "Suffering is optional." We create so much of our own suffering by reliving the past or wishing for the future, instead of simply being present and grateful when we can stay there. It's easier said than done, but it *is* possible.

. . .

I walked home from the farmers' market one night after I lost Buddy and felt my mind choosing suffering. First my mind said: "The last time I took this walk I was with Buddy." Then my mind chose to suffer in sneakier ways. As I walked I found myself thinking, "I wonder if anyone is seeing me walk by and wondering where my dog is? Will I see someone who doesn't know she died? Will someone ask me where she is?" And I choked up.

I engineered that entire train of suffering and rode it willingly. If I can redirect those thoughts in that moment, I can choose to suffer less. I would still be grieving, I would still miss her, but I don't have to suffer as much.

A fourth aspect of obedience is the discipline of self-care. It would have been easy to stop exercising, because every time I walked out the door that first week I started to cry. Missing her beside me, feeling the loss. But being disciplined and taking care of myself was part of the obedience lesson.

Eating healthy food, visiting the chiropractor, getting a massage... it would have been very easy to let all that fall away. But tapping the discipline to stay healthy is helpful.

I went to an early yoga class two days after Buddy crossed over. I hoped it would be small because I knew I would cry... but if you can't cry in yoga class, where can you cry? I took a spot in the back, hoping I wouldn't be too much of a distraction.

I make it part of my yoga practice to dedicate my class to someone. When I do this, I close my eyes and visualize the person standing in front of me on the hardwood floor. As I breathe in and breathe out, I breathe through them, sending them blessings, love and light. The class becomes a prayer for them instead of being about me and my body's limitations. I dedicated this class to Bob's healing and to Buddy Girl.

As I was meditating, Buddy appeared in front of me in my mind's eye. She wasn't standing obediently still (she never stayed put when she was alive, either); she was trotting playfully around the room, sniffing, saying hi to everyone.

Despite this, I was having a conversation with her in my meditation. (To be clear, I don't picture her talking, and I don't actually hear the words. But the thoughts come to me as clearly as if a voice was saying them.)

After 45 minutes of me crying, she finally said, "Mommy, why are you crying? I'm joy!"

And I finally smiled and said, "I know honey. I know you're joy. I'm just really sad because I miss your body being here."

And then she said, "You know, you can miss me without being sad."

You can miss me without being sad. That was going to take some work.

After class, I took my time rolling up my mat, wiping my eyes, blowing my nose. Kristin, who had been on the mat next to mine, was talking with our teacher Amanda as I approached the door. They both reached out to ask if I was okay. I told them we had lost someone. Amanda said, "As I was watching you, I thought it was your dog. I just felt a dog's energy so strongly. Was she here?"

And I said, "Yes, she was here. She was trotting around the room." And we all laughed. I said I hoped I hadn't been too distracting. Kristin told me that she spent the whole class sending me love and light. She had dedicated her class to me.

A week later I was back in class, with less crying. I dedicated the class to Bob and Buddy again. This time, Buddy was still there, but less intensely. She had less puppy energy and was more on the periphery of the room. I felt her next to me a few times when I was in Downward Dog, pushing her nose into my armpit the way she used to. At the end of class during the last meditation, the teacher told us to be the Observer, to watch ourselves. Whenever I do this, I have the same mental image.

I'm in a purple raft, floating down a river. The me in the raft is my true self, my soul, my inner light. Everything else that's in my life is floating on a log nearby. The thoughts that come into my mind are engraved on logs, and they float by. Any pain in my body is outside the raft. This detachment is the greatest gift I find in meditation, because it calms and centers me. And then I saw Buddy, in a raft just to my right. She was curled up in her raft, absolutely serene (not at all like she would have been as a real dog in a real raft). She was floating right next to me in perfect alignment, no need to have the rafts tied together. I felt at the core of my being that she would always be there, right there, no matter what. She would always be right there, because she was my girl.

As part of my obedience training I have worked on missing Buddy Girl without being sad.

Juicer pulp training biscuits—*for dogs*

Obedience training is all about the cookies, treats, or biscuits. Buddy Girl absolutely loved her cookies, and these were her favorites. Daisy loves them too. I love knowing that she is getting healthy organic biscuits. The bonus is that they are cheap and use up the pulp from your juicer. Don't have a juicer? You can also use grated vegetables.

Makes at least 75 biscuits

3 T. (*15 g*) ground flaxseeds
6 T. (*90 ml*) water
2 C. (*150 g*) gluten-free oat flour
4 C. (*700 g*) juicer pulp or shredded vegetables
1/4 C. (*60 ml*) olive oil

Preheat the oven to 350F/*160C*/*gas mark 4*. Put the flaxseeds and water in your mixing bowl and let stand 5 minutes. Add the rest of the ingredients and mix until smooth. It should be the consistency of chunk-light tuna fish salad, thick but spreadable.

Cut pieces of parchment paper to fit two rimmed baking sheets. Spray or oil the top of the paper. Spoon half the mixture onto each sheet. Put a piece of waxed paper (or a silicone sheet) on top of the mixture and use a rolling pin to roll out the dough as thinly and evenly as possible.

Gently peel back the waxed paper and repeat with the other half of the mixture. Discard the waxed paper.

Using a butter knife, score the dough, making small squares. Use your knife to neaten up any jagged edges.

Bake 20 minutes. Directions follow for finishing in the oven or in a dehydrator.

If using only an oven: Put another piece of parchment paper on top, and a fresh baking sheet face down. Flip the entire thing over, and remove the top pan and the top sheet of parchment. Turn the oven down as low as it will go, and bake until absolutely crisp. This could take 4–8 hours, depending on the thickness of the biscuits, your oven temperature, and the humidity outside. (You need to get all the moisture out of them or they will mold.)

If using a dehydrator: Let the biscuits cool enough to be handled, then break up into sections large enough to fit your trays. Dehydrate overnight at 135F/6oC. (Sometimes they take two days.)

Store in an airtight container.

Notes: Make sure you properly prep all the fruit and vegetables before using them in dog biscuits. Proper prep means:

1) Remove any seeds, especially from apples; they are toxic

2) Cut away any moldy or bruised flesh

3) Do not include avocados, grapes, mushrooms, spicy peppers, onions, tomatoes, or garlic, as they are all toxic to dogs

If your dog is on a grain-free diet, use more ground flaxseeds and enough water to get the proper consistency. These are raw if dehydrated at 115F/45C.

Community

Community

When I think about all the ways that Buddy Girl changed our lives, the first way that comes to mind is meeting our friends. Bob and I got to know more people, different people, than we ever would have met without Buddy. Daisy continues that tradition for us.

When Bob was working here in town, he walked Buddy in the mornings while I walked her in the afternoons. He had a secret life with her, meeting particular people, going his own special route. And along the way, Bob and Buddy met Gail, a retired lady who lives a few blocks away.

At the time, Gail had a routine of walking with two other women around the neighborhood and she always had dog treats with her. As she got to know Buddy, she fell in love with her. She later told me that Buddy was the first dog she ever bonded with.

Once Bob began to work out of town, I did both the morning and the evening walks. It was funny for the first few months, because I would run into people in the mornings who would greet Buddy with open arms, and then look up at me and say in an accusing tone, "Who are YOU?" I'd reply, "I'm the mom."

I soon discovered that Buddy's route involved cookies. If we went out the front door and turned to the left (her preference), then she would drag me to the market for a Milkbone. If we went right (my preference), she would inevitably get me to walk past Gail's, where she would drag me up the steps to knock on the door and wait for cookies.

If it was Monday morning, the high school booster room door would be open, and the volunteer moms had cookies too. Once Bud realized that, she slowed to a stop every time we passed that doorway, even when I would tug on her leash and say, "She's not here today honey. No cookies!" I have never seen a dog have a relationship with an entire neighborhood, but Buddy did.

Sometimes in the morning I'd be working or in the bathroom and I'd hear her barking: crazy, someone's-at-the-door barking. Most times, I'd go to the door and there would be no one there. It drove me nuts.

One day I realized that there was a Milkbone balanced on the screen-door handle. Gail was now delivering cookies to my dog.

As we got to know Gail, we learned that her husband was an invalid, bedridden in their home. One day I asked if he would like to meet Buddy. We went into his bedroom and she trotted up to him and gently licked his arm while he petted her. He responded to Buddy in a beautiful way, and after that, Gail was more than Cookie Lady. She was a friend. When Gail's husband died a few months later, we would stop and give Gail a hug and she would cuddle with Buddy for a while.

Part of what happens when you get a dog is figuring out who is going to take care of it when you have to leave town. While we did board Buddy Girl a few times, for the most part we traded off with neighbors. The dog-sitting trade-off can be a tricky proposition. You have to pick people who you know will take good care of your dog, as well as ones whose dog you would actually be willing to take yourself. They have to be people who will reciprocate in an easy manner, otherwise the relationship becomes unbalanced. And they have to be mellow enough that if your dog eats, say, a favorite hat or bra, this transgression won't sour your relationship. Like I said: it's tricky.

Bob and I are incredibly blessed to have many such friends, and Buddy Girl was a favorite in the neighborhood. We actually had enough people who liked to watch her that I could rotate through them, so as not to overstay her welcome at any one house.

In return, that meant we had dogs stay with us fairly regularly. Hops stayed over the most, but we also had Annie, Star, Bizzy, and Leo. Having a second dog around brings your dog into focus. You realize that you're doing a good job with one aspect of their training, but are maybe not so great in another area. And overall you like

your dog a whole lot better than anyone else's dog. Which is as it should be, as the same set of thoughts undoubtedly go through your friends' minds when your dog is with them.

I called Hops, Annie, Star, Bizzy, and Leo my loaner dogs. I always enjoyed having them, and was always relieved to see them go. For one thing, you hope that nothing happens to them on your watch. You also realize how much more work it is to take care of two dogs: eight paws to clean, two bowls to wash, two coats to brush, a million times more hair to Swiff up.

You learn a lot about your friends, sometimes things you'd rather not know. Perhaps they forgot to mention that they get up at 5 am every day to go running with their dog. Or that their dog drinks out of the toilet, or will eat stuff out of the trash can, or expects to sleep on the bed. Or their dog rushes the front door, or inexplicably attacks a particular spot on the lawn and becomes obsessed with it.

Meanwhile, your dog collects their baby's socks, in pairs, and carries the socks delicately around the house. She roots out every single missing ball from behind their furniture, which their own dog has completely forgotten about, obsessively whining until every last one is unearthed. She is tolerant of their kids and their cats, but draws the line at their chickens.

Right after Buddy Girl died, I needed to keep up my daily walks, both for fitness and to get out of the house, but I couldn't bear to walk alone. I started picking up Hops, my neighbor's Golden. Hops is a big, goofy boy, who is BEYOND excited to go for a walk. He's impossible to walk without a prong collar, but he's good company. People would see me in the neighborhood, do a double take, and I'd say, "This is Hops. He's a loaner." Hops was a godsend, that doofus-y boy, who was not-Buddy but enough of Buddy to make the walks bearable. And I loved him a little bit more for it, despite him being a loaner.

2001 was Buddy's first Halloween. It became her favorite holiday, if I can be so bold as to put that un-doglike thought into her head. She was very willing to wear a costume, so long as it did not involve a hat or any hat-like object. Dog trainers say that wearing costumes is great preparation for dogs, should they ever need to wear bandages or the cone of shame.

Bob was responsible for the first costume, her cowgirl outfit. After we ran out of candy we walked her around the neighborhood, trick-or-treating for biscuits at doggie friends' houses. She didn't love walking in the costume, or being around all the people in costumes and masks, but she tolerated the whole experience quite well.

What she did love were the kids. About a month before Halloween I would start thinking about her costume... what would suit her, what would look cute, what would entertain the kids. We dressed her up so that we could be that fun house on the block with the dog in a costume, as a counterpoint to the ten scary houses with the screaming soundtrack and the ghouls jumping out of the bushes.

If she had hated it, she could have hung out in the bedroom all night and we never would have done it again. But she seemed to love it. We set up a baby gate at the front door so she could stand there and welcome wave after wave of kids. We get nearly 400 trick-or-treaters every year, so it's a long night. We'd hear them from the sidewalk, "Oh, the dog is dressed up! You have to come see it!" And she would stand there all night long, wagging her tail and swishing her skirt, greeting everyone who came to see her.

One year she was Snow White, and many a Disney princess came to the door and giggled at the sight of her furry twin. She was a ballerina, and a cheerleader, and on her last Halloween, a lovely sunflower.

I had no idea whether Daisy would love or hate Halloween, and was happy to discover that she didn't even notice the costume, and happily hung out all night next to me at the front door, sitting quietly to be petted by the hundreds of kids. I also found out that many people looked forward to Buddy Girl and remembered her from past Halloweens, and were sad to learn she was gone. I'm glad that we're still the house with the dog in a costume.

Maple-pecan glazed popcorn—*for people*

I like to make this sweet-and-salty snack to eat during our three-hour night of trick-or-treaters. It keeps me out of the candy dish, satisfying any cravings I have for treats.

Makes 10–12 servings

3 T. (*45 ml*) canola, safflower, or grapeseed oil
1/2 C. (*100 g*) popcorn kernels
1 C. (*100 g*) pecan halves or pieces
3 T. (*45 ml*) agave syrup
2 T. (*30 ml*) maple syrup
1 T. (*15 g*) vegan butter
1 1/2 t. (*3 g*) smoked salt
1/2 t. (*1 g*) cinnamon
1/4 t. each (*0.5 g*) ground cloves, nutmeg, and allspice

Preheat oven to 300F/*150C/gas mark 2*.

Coat two large rimmed baking sheets with parchment paper, and spray the paper with cooking spray. Coat the inside of a large mixing bowl with cooking spray.

Pour oil in a large saucepan with a lid over high heat and cover with a lid. Keep a close eye on it so it doesn't start smoking. When the oil is shimmering, toss in one or two kernels. The oil is ready when they sizzle and bounce around.

Add the rest of the popcorn, cover the pan, and shake it vigorously to coat the kernels in hot oil.

Keep shaking it every minute or two until the popcorn starts to pop rapidly. When the popping slows down to once every two or three seconds, remove it from the heat.

Pour the popcorn into the bowl and add the nuts.

In a small saucepan over medium heat, bring the maple syrup, butter, salt, and spices just to a boil.

Pour syrup over popcorn and nuts, stirring to coat.

Transfer popcorn mixture to the baking sheets. Bake for 30 minutes, stirring every 10 minutes.

Remove from oven and cool on wire racks. Break into small clusters. Store in an airtight container.

Adventure

WHAT A GREAT BACK YARD !

Adventure

As you get older, it becomes easier and easier to chicken out. You skip the party, avoid the new restaurant, narrowing down the risk in your life experiences. You decline the trek across the border, the skydiving invitation, and the spontaneous road trip. You always cite a great reason, but the sparkle fades from your life.

Dogs can bring out the best in us, remind us to slow down, take a break, sit on the grass. They also push us into new situations, ones that might be out of our comfort zone. You become friends with people you would never, ever talk to otherwise. You roam through your neighborhood at odd hours. You learn to avoid where the skunks are. You're aware of when the sun rises and sets. You sit on the grass. You take your shoes off.

· · ·

I adore the picture of baby Buddy Girl, who loved to pounce into our nasturtiums. She would sidle down underneath them waiting for us to walk by and then spring out: *Gotcha!* It was a sad day for us when she became too big for that game.

Daisy likes to *eat* the nasturtiums, and one day I caught her leaping up and trying to eat our tall yellow California irises. To puppies, like babies, everything is new. While having to teach them every single aspect of life can be trying, it's also a wonderful gift.

Bob and I became bolder people because of Buddy Girl, and that boldness is now part of us. We talk to complete strangers. Bob said that having a dog is like truth serum, opening people up and lowering our inhibitions. It's true. We give our phone number to strangers in order to have a puppy play date. We innately trust dog people. We stay at places we otherwise might not, because they are dog friendly. We eat at restaurants with patios. We walk instead of drive.

This newfound boldness led me to start a food blog and a brand new career at age 50, when many people are just dreaming about retirement. It helped me say yes to ziplining at a friend's house when I might have said no.

Having a puppy brings it all back: the newness of life, the excitement in a flower, the attraction of a bee flying by or an ant on the ground. Life is ripe with exploration and adventure.

Buddy Girl's nasturtium salad with honey-poppy-seed dressing—*for people*

One of our favorite memories of Buddy is her leaping into a mound of nasturtiums. If you've never eaten edible flowers, they make a show-stopping addition to salads. Nasturtiums are strongly peppery, so I created a sweet and smoky dressing to balance the flavors. It tastes a lot like bottled French dressing. Cucumbers provide some welcome fresh crunch.

Makes 6–8 servings, or as needed

Honey-poppy-seed dressing
Makes 1-1/2 C. (*375 ml*)

1/2 C. (*125 ml*) safflower, canola, or
  grapeseed oil
1/2 C. (*125 ml*) honey
1/4 C. (*60 ml*) apple cider vinegar
1/4 C. (*60 ml*) fresh lemon juice
1 T. (*5 g*) poppy seeds
1 t. (*2 g*) smoked paprika (*pimenton*)

Warm the honey so it's very runny and thin.
I usually microwave water in a heat-proof
container, then sit the honey jar in the water.
Add to all the other ingredients in a jar with a
tightly fitting lid. Shake until well blended.

For each salad:
1 large handful each red and green oak
  leaf lettuce
1/2 cucumber
3–5 nasturtium flowers
drizzle of dressing

Wash and spin dry the lettuce.

Peel and slice the cucumber.

Harvest the nasturtium flowers right before
serving. Wash gently by immersing in water,
then spin dry. Check inside and on the stem for
critters. If you see any black specks, they are
bugs. Remove them with a toothpick.

Pile the lettuce on your serving plates, adding
6 or 8 slices of cucumber and 3–5 flowers per
plate. Serve with the dressing.

Courage

Courage

I was doing yoga on the Thursday morning after Christmas 2011. Bud finally got up and came and lay next to me for a while. Then she went to her spot in the kitchen. She had had a weird cough for days, like she was trying to puke something up. She started coughing again that morning and didn't stop until she'd coughed up some clots of blood. We didn't know it then, but there are very few things that make a dog cough up blood. They are all bad.

We saw the vet at 11:00. The vet listened to her breathing and was concerned to hear wheezing. She took Bud into the back for chest x-rays. While we waited, not knowing that we were in the last minutes of normalcy, I tried not to imagine the worst.

It wasn't until we walked back into the exam room and saw the x-ray that we knew it was bad. A large tumor lay next to her heart, and countless small circles spotted her chest cavity, all tumors. The vet suggested that we get abdominal x-rays and have a radiologist look at them to make sure, as there were one or two remote possibilities it could be something other than terminal cancer. We nodded, shell-shocked, as we waited for more x-rays. The abdominal x-rays were worse. Her whole abdomen was full of fluid, which explained why she looked to be

her normal weight, but was six pounds lighter than usual.

Our no-nonsense vet had tears in her eyes when she came back in, explaining the x-rays, and preparing us for what to expect. Buddy Girl could have a few days or a few weeks. There was no way to tell. The cancer was fast and aggressive. We would have to make a decision soon. She sent us home for the New Year's weekend and we agreed to call her early the next week. Her last words to us were, "You're going to have to be very brave."

. . .

That day and the next two were tortuous. We stayed home, hunkered down, watching her. Now that we knew what was wrong, we saw how hard she was working to breathe: fast and shallow. We saw how low her energy was. We watched her cough with a towel at hand, holding it under her mouth to catch any blood. The coughing didn't happen very often, but when it did we ached with her. We cancelled our New Year's Day brunch on Sunday, sending out a short note letting friends know that Buddy was sick, inviting her special friends to stop by soon if they wanted a last visit with her.

By Saturday I knew that we had very little time. She didn't want to get up, and didn't leave the bedroom until her favorite Cookie Lady Gail came by to see her. She came into the living room and lay down on the floor next to Gail, who pet her for nearly an hour. You could tell Bud felt miserable.

It was hard to actually say it, to start making the plans to end her life. We called our neighbor Suzi, an ER vet, and asked if she could come by on Sunday morning to advise us.

. . .

Sunday morning dawned clear and bright, and it was tempting to hope. We always pray before meals, so we dedicated the day to Buddy and her friends, trusting that the people who were meant to come by would do so, asking that she have a good day, asking for grace.

Suzi came over and checked Buddy out. Based on what she was seeing and what we'd told her, she thought she had a rare cancer called hemangiosarcoma. It starts in the blood vessels and spreads quickly throughout the body, creating tumors in the organs. She said that dogs like Buddy Girl, who are so bright and happy, will do everything they can to mask how terrible they are feeling, people pleasers until the end. And she might have some good minutes or

hours, but over the balance of the day, she'd be feeling pretty miserable, maybe 30 good minutes out of every 24 hours. And then, God bless her, Suzi said what we needed to hear:

"Don't wait. It's not going to get any easier. Especially with this cancer... she could die very suddenly if her lungs start to hemorrhage, which would be devastating for all of you."

What an incredibly loving, compassionate gift Suzi gave us. Because once we made the decision, it wasn't torture any more. We knew what we had to do. We were in excruciating pain but we weren't tortured by indecision or doubt.

She laid out our options: home, your vet, the animal ER... so that we could think through what would feel the best to us. After she left we decided to call the next day and to take Bud to a clinic we knew, where the vets were super-compassionate but didn't have a relationship with us. I knew that there was no way I could bear watching our vet—who had been with us since day one—lay Buddy to rest.

. . .

Once we accepted the reality, the rest of that day was such a sweet gift. As people started coming over, Bud rallied. She pulled her toys out; she trotted around, showing off her party scarf; she played a little. When Gail came to visit again, Buddy was turning around in circles wagging her tail, and Gail asked where she was. The contrast was so great from the day before that Gail didn't even recognize her. Bud was so excited to see everyone, even though many of the humans were inexplicably crying. We put the box of tissues on the table and stopped trying to hold back our tears.

It was an incredible testament to the kind of beauty Buddy was—a light-filled joyous being. So many people came by that day to say goodbye. Our culture deals with death so poorly. We sanitize it; we hide it away; we compartmentalize grief. We don't want to deal with an impending death, so we pretend it isn't happening, instead of mustering the courage to have the brave conversations.

What Buddy's last days taught me was how powerful it can be to embrace this end-of-life experience and make it holy, to celebrate the end of a life as much as we do the beginning.

It was beautiful to have people cry with us. Does that sound weird? It was beautiful. If you're not a dog person, you might think it's odd. How can people feel that much for an animal? I assure you, it's the easiest thing on earth.

Buddy's spirit was such a beautiful light in the world, and many of these friends had watched her when we were out of town. They had their own relationship with her. They had fed her and played with her and walked her. She had slept by their beds, cuddled with their kids, wrestled with their dogs. Buddy had so many friends.

By late afternoon everyone had gone and Bud was pooped. She slept by the front door, her head on the sill, getting some fresh air. Bob and I marked time working on piddling computer projects.

I was wiped out and we decided to lie down together as a family, so Bob lifted Bud up onto the bed for the first authorized time in her life.

As I lay next to her, stroking her soft fur, I could hear how hard it was for her to breathe. She wasn't gasping or laboring, but the breaths were fast and exaggerated. I asked Bob if he thought we should take her in right away. He was sure she was okay for one more night.

It was hard not to think about the next day and how much I was going to miss her, but Bob was great about reminding me to be present.

· · ·

At dusk we took her for a little walk around the neighborhood. First we went to the market around the corner, where they always gave out the huge Milkbones. We let her choose the route, and she took us to Gail's house (surprise!) for more cookies. But Gail wasn't home, so we kept walking. Our friends Nicole and Matt were out front unloading their car. They got to say goodbye and gave us hugs. Their dogs Bear and Jessie came out to greet their pal Buddy as well.

We ran into Suzi the vet with her family and Gail one last time. We went by the park where Buddy had played and run so many times. We stopped at her favorite pine tree and found some good juicy pinecones for her. I sat on the grass and watched her methodically tear up one after another after another.

She was incredibly deliberate about it, holding them upright between her paws, using her dewclaws like thumbs. She never ate the pinecones. She methodically ripped off each individual cone and spit them out, leaving nothing but a thin core and a pile of cones.

It was dark and time to head home.

· · ·

We came home with her feet all filthy, and I cleaned her off with baby wipes. I had been saying for more than a week how she needed a bath and her paws were a mess. She would have to go to heaven dirty and ungroomed. I was trying not to let it bug me, to let it go, knowing that it wasn't important, knowing that it didn't mean she wasn't loved. I knew in my heart that I was focusing on something unimportant to distract myself from this big thing that *was* happening.

I made her a special dinner of chicken and veggies and kibble and fed her by hand. At bedtime, Bob put her up on the bed again for a while, so we could cuddle with her one last time. She had a good, quiet last night in her bed on the floor next to me, with no coughing spells.

Chamomile-ginger tea—*for people*

Makes 2 cups of courage

2 chamomile tea bags
2 ginger tea bags or several slices of fresh ginger
1 lemon
2–3 T. (*30–45 ml*) honey

Bring two cups of water to a boil, then pour into a teapot with the tea bags, ginger, and honey. Squeeze the lemon juice into the teapot. Let steep for five minutes before serving.

If you have to gird your loins to do the difficult, this drink will help. The ginger settles your stomach while the honey, lemon, and chamomile soothe your soul.

Mindfulness

Mindfulness

We were listening to some of Deepak Chopra's short meditations when Bud came into the kitchen on her last day. She was quiet, a little tired and stiff from all the visitors the day before. Since she seemed okay and we had good weather, we decided to spend the day outside in her favorite place.

I called the vet and set our appointment for 3:15 to give us as much time as possible. We ate a little bit, showered, and packed up her bag with snacks, water, treats, and toys. I fed her cookies with peanut butter on them, as she wasn't very hungry for breakfast. I had made a big batch of her juicer-pulp cookies the week before, and I realized that I didn't need to save them. Buddy could finish them off.

Bob said, "If you think of each thing as being the last time, we're never going to get through this day. We just have to stay present and breathe."

My favorite breathing mantra from yoga is *Om* on the in-breath, *Shanti* on the out-breath. *Om* has many meanings, but "God" is one of them. *Shanti* means peace. It's my go-to mantra, and I used it the entire day.

We took the blanket from her bed for the back seat of the car; I knew I wouldn't want it back. She was wearing her little party scarf, we'd given her a quick brushing, and she finally had her pretty paws after my trimming that morning. As usual, she was excited to go for a ride.

I rode in the back seat with her, which was so unusual that she kept shifting around uncertainly. I wanted to hug and pet her as much as I could. We got to Coronado Island around 10:30. The rest of that day I didn't pay attention to time, until it was time to go.

The amazing thing about that day, and the incredible last gift Buddy gave us, was the pure lesson in mindfulness. As long as I could stay in the present, look at the ocean, see the little kids respond to her, enjoy watching her sniff, or splash around at the water's edge, I could appreciate everything I was seeing.

And the time miraculously expanded.

The second I started thinking about 3:15, or "the last time we…" then the tears would start to well up, my throat would start to close, and time would shrink. I worked all day long at being present. I did a lot of *Om/shanti's*, which was the only way that I could keep my mind from going somewhere excruciatingly sad. As long as I didn't go there, the day was gorgeously perfect.

We went for a long walk with lots of stops and sniffing, her absolute favorite thing to do. We let her splash in the water on the leash. While she would have loved to swim, we knew that would be too much for her. We stopped frequently to rest, sniff, pet her, and take pictures. Initially it seemed odd to take pictures, but I am so glad that we did. It was an absolutely brilliant day, sunny and crisp, and tons of people stopped and said hi to her.

We fed her apple slices with peanut butter on them and carrots and she got to watch skateboarders at the skate park. She was alert and very present.

We made our way back to the ferry landing and ordered some lunch. For the first time ever, I fed her french fries from my lunch. Bob said, "Well, it's not the first time she's had French fries..." and we both laughed. We fed her chicken kabobs and grilled shrimp and let her drink out of our cup. I didn't care. I wondered if people were looking at us and judging us, not knowing what was happening. My friend Marjorie told me that she'd done the exact same thing, feeding raw filet mignon to her dog Sally on Sally's last day.

We moseyed over to the spot where Bob had proposed to me more than a decade ago, and found some nice grass that was sheltered from the wind. We lay there on the grass for a while. The sky was so blue, and Bud looked beautiful. Her fur was glowing in the light, and as I looked up at her, her nostrils were almost translucent, backlit by the bright sun. I knew that she was working hard to breathe, but she was also so present, so alert. She was calm, watching every single thing that was happening.

We asked some tourists to take our picture. For them, we were simply a middle-aged couple with their older dog. I get choked up when I think about what that picture was for us: our last family photo. But at the time, Bob and I were both smiling. We managed to be present. Bud is glowing, probably just a trick of the sunlight; to me she looks like she was already partly spirit.

We did some more moseying, got a drink, and then it felt like we were killing time. Bud started coughing and green mucus started coming out of her mouth. She threw up some french fries. It was time to go.

The drive to the vet's was tough, because we knew where we were going, what was going to happen, and it felt like lying to her. But I never doubted that we were doing the right thing.

The vet's staff members were great. They had a room ready for us and took us straight in, they explained everything clearly and compassionately; they respected our wishes and our time with her.

As we were waiting for the vet to bring her back into the room with her catheter in, Bob asked me how I wanted this to go. Did I want a lot of time with her? I said no. We prayed and blessed the room. And he said, very seriously, "Now I don't want her staying here. She's so attached to you. I want her to cross over. You have to tell her to cross over. She'll listen to you."

I told him, "She and I have had this conversation many times. She knows that she has to come back, so of course she needs to cross over. But I'll tell her again."

They brought Buddy in and gave us just five minutes at our request. We got her to lie down on the blanket, kneeling beside her. We had been saying goodbye to her in a sacred space all day and we didn't want this hard part to last any longer than it needed to. Here's what we told Buddy Girl:

"We know you're really tired and you don't feel well. It's time for you to go to sleep. All of your doggie friends are waiting for you. You're going to see them in a beautiful white light: Hannah and Bizzy and Zuma and Zincey and Thoren. We want you to go to them. We want you to cross over. It's okay to leave us. It's time to cross over."

And then the vet came in and explained that there would be three shots, and that it would happen very quickly. One would relax her; one would stop her heart. It would be very peaceful.

I honestly don't know how they do it. When two grown people are on their knees sobbing, how do vets do their jobs? But I'm grateful for it, too. What I didn't expect was how shockingly fast it was. 30 seconds? A minute?

What I do know is that Buddy Girl was definitively gone. Her beautiful, soft body was lying there, like she was in a deep sleep, but her spirit was absolutely gone. The vet told us that we might see some muscles twitching, but it was just reflex. They left us alone. She was absolutely still. We kissed her one more time, took her collar,

and we headed home to a silent house to grieve.

As we prayed about her in the days afterwards, we always imagined her spirit in heaven. Bob kept saying he imagined that she's the greeter, joyfully meeting people as they cross over. I took comfort in thinking that she was there to meet our friend Pete, not even waiting for him to cross all the way over, but tearing down that bright tunnel and meeting him halfway, spinning around at his knees as she always did. We do hope that at some point she will come back.

When I think about her last two days, I feel so blessed. Blessed to have a partner who was such a rock. Blessed to have such incredible friends. Blessed to have shared that with Buddy Girl.

How amazing if all of us could have one day at the end of our lives where our dearest friends came by, spent time with us, told us how much they loved us, and tenderly said goodbye. We could eat all of our favorite foods, no matter how bad they were for us. And on our last day, we got to go to our absolute favorite place, spend the whole day outside doing our favorite things with the people we love most, and then when it was time, went to sleep in 30 seconds and off to heaven where all of our friends are waiting for us. Would that we all had such a beautiful ending.

Oven fries with homemade balsamic ketchup—*for people and very good dogs*

Life's too short to eat junk food, but don't we all crave fries once in a while? Imagine Buddy's joy at getting to share these with you.

Serves several people and one Golden retriever

(Use one large potato per person)
4 organic russet potatoes
1 T. (*15 ml*) organic extra-virgin olive oil
1 small sprig of fresh rosemary
1/2 t. (*1 g*) sea salt

Pre-heat the oven to *425F/220C/gas mark 6.5.*

Cut a piece of parchment paper to fit a large rimmed baking sheet.

Scrub the potatoes and let dry.

Wash and thoroughly dry the rosemary. Pull off all the needles, and mince as finely as you can. Using the back of a spoon, mash the rosemary into the salt in a bowl until it releases its fragrance.

Slice the potatoes lengthwise in half, then quarters, then eighths. Your goal is to have uniform spears, so try to use potatoes that are the same size and shape. If you end up with a few thicker pieces, cut them in half again lengthwise.

Dump the potatoes into your biggest kitchen bowl and drizzle the oil over them, stirring to coat thoroughly. Sprinkle with half of the sea salt mixture.

Spread the potatoes across the baking sheet, making sure they are not stuck together.

Bake for a total of 45 minutes, stirring at 15 and 30 minutes, or until the potatoes are golden brown on the outside, soft and fluffy inside.

Sprinkle with the remaining sea salt, or to taste.

Serve with balsamic ketchup to dip. Ignore the pleading brown eyes as long as you can.

If you do feed these to your dog, don't give them ketchup; tomatoes and onion aren't safe for dogs.

Balsamic ketchup

Makes 1-1/2 C. (*375 ml*)
1 T. (*15 ml*) extra-virgin olive oil
1/2 medium red onion (*60 g*)
1 garlic clove
14.5 oz. (*400-425 g*) canned organic tomato puree or tomato pieces, no salt added
1/4 C. (*40 g*) organic coconut sugar or brown sugar
2 T. (*30 ml*) balsamic vinegar
1/2 t. (*1 g*) kosher salt
1/4 t. (*0.5 g*) ground mustard
pinch of ground cloves

Peel and roughly chop the onion. Peel and mince the garlic clove.

Heat the olive oil over medium heat in a heavy-bottomed deep saucepan or pot, then add the onions. Cook about 9 minutes, until translucent and starting to caramelize. Add the garlic and cook 1 minute.

Add the remaining ingredients and bring to a bubble, stirring. Turn down the heat until just barely simmering and partially cover. Cook for one hour.

Blend the mixture in a blender until completely smooth. Be careful when transferring to the blender, and hold down the blender top with a kitchen towel while you blend, as the hot mixture will rapidly expand and release steam.

If it is not thick enough, put it back into the pot and continue to cook on low another 15–30 minutes, stirring occasionally, until it is ketchup consistency. Use a funnel to pour into clean glass bottles (it takes a while to drip through).

Refrigerate and use within a month.

Release

Release

My friend Alex, who is from Colima, Mexico, tells me that dogs are revered in her culture because of their role in the afterlife. She was taught that when you die you cross a river to get to the underworld. The river can be treacherous and not everyone makes it. Dogs have the sacred duty of guiding you across.

In one version of heaven in my mind, Buddy was heaven's greeter. She wasn't waiting at some rainbow-colored bridge. She had a job: to be the sunshine girl that she always was, greeting every single person who comes through that tunnel of light into heaven. Oh man, would she love that job. She was born for that job.

When Buddy was a puppy and we would go to the dog park, she would romp around and play, but she always had one eye on the parking lot. The instant that anyone arrived at the dog park and hit the grass, Bud would prance her little wiggle-bottom over there to greet them. She wasn't all that interested in the dogs, but every single person needed to be greeted with a wag and kiss. One time she ran up to a new guy, and he reached down and hugged her and said, "Well, you're just a big baby aren't you? Just a big ol' baby!" She would sit on the feet of special friends, leaning against them to be petted.

In my other version of heaven, Bud played with some with her friends, got a few good hard puppy wrestles in, and then she ran right up to the counter to sign up to come back, because she knows we really need her. I guess, time in the afterlife not being linear, she could do both.

* * *

Either way, we had to release her. Release is peculiar. To truly love someone you have to set them free. You have to let them be themselves, love them for who they are, embrace their beautiful qualities, and release any outcome.

That is a challenge.

When you are bonded to a dog, you know that the day will come when you'll have to let her go. You know it, yet you live in denial her whole life. The more you love her, the more you know the end is going to hurt. And it would have been so tempting to hold onto Buddy, to put it off another day, and another day. Because she was doing her best to hide how poorly she was feeling.

At the same time, I do hope she'll come back one day, and I like to think that she hand-picked Daisy this time around, another lovely soul in a dog suit to join our family.

Part of grieving is release. Releasing your sadness, releasing your tears, releasing the ache. Embrace it when it reappears, and then release it again.

Part of my releasing Buddy was figuring out meaningful ways to honor her. Writing this book, creating a two-page letter we emailed out, announcing the news on Facebook, announcing it on my blog. Each was difficult, as each announcement created a new wave of sympathy. Each sweet condolence message made me cry, and yet it was part of how I could release her. We created a simple announcement card that we had printed on nice heavy paper, and planned her little memorial service. We bought a beautiful baby Meyer lemon tree with an engraved tag for it. Meyer lemons are sweet, juicy, full of sunshine. I love the idea of thinking of her every time I use lemons from her tree. We've already named it Little Miss Sunshine.

In the months between Buddy's leaving and Daisy's arrival, the first thing I would do when I woke up was picture Buddy lying on her bed on the floor to my left, her paws over her head, her back legs splayed out. I would say good morning to her and feel that happiness and joy that she always brought me. Then I would roll over and look to my left at the empty wooden floor. No bed, no dog. That's the release. I could tap into my Buddy Girl happiness any time, and choose not to feel sad.

. . .

We spent time thinking about what to do with Bud's ashes. We wanted them back. It didn't seem right to leave her at the vet's to be disposed of, so we requested a private cremation. Someone comes and picks up your dog's body and takes it to their facility, where they prepare and cremate the body. If you don't ask for a private cremation they do a group cremation and bury the ashes there.

After a week I went back to the vet to pick up the "cremains." They were in a nice gift bag, with themed tissue and a wooden tag with her name on it. The pet cemetery provided small, thoughtful mementos to keep: an envelope of fur, a paw print in clay, a little ornament you could keep for your Christmas tree, a cedar lockbox with an engraved name plate. I was surprised at how heavy the bag was, but of course she was a 70-pound dog, even at the end. You think of ashes as being light, but inside the cedar lock box was a bag of dense grey sand. It took me several weeks to be able to look inside.

It's so weird to think of a body turning into sand or ash. Bob and I both want to be cremated. I don't even want to spend the money on embalming; just get it over with. But now I understand that it helps others through their grieving process to be able to view the body and say goodbye. With a dog, since you choose their last day, you can do that when they are alive.

We didn't want to bury Buddy in our yard, because I thought it would be too sad to think of her there every day. We talked about her favorite beach, but I didn't like the idea of spreading her on the water or putting her into the sand.

Then we thought about her favorite park, where she had spent so many weekends and evenings running, playing, and chewing up pinecones. That was it. The pine tree. We decided we would bury her ashes under her favorite tree, so she would always be part of that tree and the pinecones, and also close to the dogs and little kids she loved so much.

We can walk over there any time and sit and remember her.

· · ·

On a beautiful day in late February, just around sunset, we invited some special friends to join us. The week leading up to her ceremony was hard. Even though she'd been dead for nearly two months, there's something final about a burial. I knew it was part of the letting go and that we needed to do it in order to move on, but of course I just wanted her back.

I searched for something to read at the ceremony and finally settled on the lyrics from U2's song Magnificent, which was part of my walking playlist in the first weeks after she crossed over. I wrote a little outline for the ceremony and talked it over with Bob. He had some things he wanted to say, and I wanted

to read the lyric, and then we would invite our guests to share a memory.

We didn't want the ceremony to be sad, but even after two months I was sad planning it, and as the week went by I felt more and more weepy. I played the song I had chosen for the actual burial over and over, hoping that hearing it repeatedly would desensitize me, but still it made me cry. I read the lyrics over and over, and still they made me cry.

I loaded photos of Buddy onto my iPad for the slide show. That made me cry. And so it went. I had planned on making pine nut biscotti and dog biscuits as the refreshments, thinking it would tickle Bud to know I had somehow worked her pinecones into the theme.

I made honey lemonade using Meyer lemons, which reminded me of her Little Miss Sunshine tree.

We spent time thinking about what to use to scoop the ashes and dig the holes, as Bob wanted her ashes to encircle the tree. Bob was adamant that he not use a "dirty old shovel" to dig the holes. We found a heavy silver scoop at a kitchen store and Bob picked out a new hand spade for the holes. I made a list, and started putting things into a bag.

We had received more than two dozen sympathy cards, and I thought it would be sweet to incorporate them into the event. I punched holes in them and strung them on purple ribbon, along with the printouts of the dozens of emails we received. They hung from the tree like prayer flags fluttering in the wind, surrounding us with love.

While Bob dug the holes, I decorated a table with her photos on the iPad, the cedar box, the scoop, the refreshments, a candle that refused to stay lit, her paw print, and a small vase of flowers from the yard. I chose nasturtiums—they reminded me of her as a puppy—plus other sunny, happy, bright flowers. I had the tin of biscotti, the jar of doggie biscuits, and a basket full of her dog toys to share.

Sixteen friends and five dogs joined us, and it was lovely. Bob did a wonderful job starting things off, talking about how Buddy brought so many friends into our lives, so much love. We invited friends to share a Buddy story, and we heard how much she meant to them, and especially how much their kids loved her too. I did cry when reading the lyrics, but that's okay. Everyone helped with the ashes, even the little kids, which was sweet.

Then we ate and drank a little, wrapping up as the sun dropped and the weather got chilly. Packing up felt like closure, another step towards healing.

· · ·

We had met with an alternative healer that morning and she said something that struck me as perfect for this day. "We think of the earth as solid and still, but the earth is actually spinning quite fast, both on its axis and around the sun. And there are all these other heavenly bodies spinning around us. And the entire solar system is now thought to be spinning around another sun. So every single thing is constantly in motion, in change."

We can't control change, and if we try, we make ourselves miserable. But if we can simply flow with it, knowing all is in motion, that's when we can feel at ease. And now Buddy is both in motion and at rest under a tree, returning to the earth as we all do.

Lemon-pine nut biscotti—*for people*

I made these crunchy cookies for Buddy's ceremony. They combine her Meyer-lemon-sunshine-girl essence with her favorite pine coney-ness.

Makes about 20 cookies

2 T. (*12 g*) flax seeds—or 2 eggs
4 T. (*60 ml*) filtered water (omit if using eggs)
1 C. (*150 g*) gluten-free flour mix
1/2 C. (*60 g*) almond meal
1/3 C. (*63 g*) cornmeal
2/3 C. (*100 g*) pine nuts
1 T. (*5 g*) baking powder
1/2 t. (*1 g*) salt
2/3 C. (*100 g*) coconut sugar
1/3 C. (*80 ml*) extra-virgin olive oil
1/4 C. (*60 ml*) lemon juice
1/4 C. (*60 ml*) soy milk
zest from the lemons

Preheat oven to 350F/*180C/gas mark 4*.
Cover a large baking sheet with parchment paper. Spray lightly with cooking spray.
Grind the flax seeds in a blender until they are a fine meal. Add them to a medium-sized mixing bowl with the water and let sit for at least five minutes to gel. Skip this step if using eggs.
Sift or whisk together the flour, almond meal, cornmeal, sugar, salt, and baking powder together into a large bowl. Whisk in the pine nuts.

Whisk the oil, sugar, lemon juice, soy milk, and lemon zest into the smaller bowl with the flax seeds or eggs.

Stir the wet ingredients into the dry ingredients until evenly mixed and a soft dough forms. Take half of the dough and form a narrow log running the length of the baking sheet. You can use the paper to fold it over and help shape it.

Repeat with the other half of the dough. These cookies don't rise very much.

Bake for 25–30 minutes until golden brown and firm on top.

Remove from the oven and let cool on the baking sheet atop a wire rack for 15-20 minutes.

Reset the oven temperature to 325F/*165C/ gas mark 3*.

Remove the logs from the baking sheet to a large cutting board. Using a serrated knife, slice them crosswise or on the diagonal into 1/2-inch-thick (*1.25 cm*) slices. Return them to the baking sheet cut side down.

Bake for 15 minutes then flip them over. Bake another 15 minutes. Flip again. Bake for a final 10 minutes until golden brown and crunchy.

Transfer to a wire rack to cool completely. Store in an airtight metal tin.

Joy

Joy

This was my Buddy Girl, and this was the face I called my shiny penny. She would trot into the kitchen in the mornings and look up at me with her happy, bright face, and I'd say, "There's my shiny penny!"

She had a million nicknames. Her name started out as simply Buddy. When we registered her with the AKC (just because we could), she was "Buddy of Bancroft Street." Because she was a really big girl with a broad chest and a blue collar, everyone thought she was a boy. So we started introducing her as Buddy Girl.

She was also Buddleia (the taxonomic name for butterfly bush), BG, Buddelia Rose (especially when she was in trouble with mom), Bud Bud, Puppy Love, Boo Boo, Boo Boo Girl, Puppas, Puppa Puppa, Mrs. Wigglebottoms, Mrs. W.B., Wanker, Wanktankerous, Sleepy McSleeperson, Princess, Your Majesty, Snaggletooth, Sweet Pea, and many more. She was our Little Miss Sunshine, and she embodied joy.

When she would come into the kitchen in the morning, I would bow to her and say, "Good morning, Your Majesty" and she would bow back.

. . .

Look into some dogs' eyes, and they are… blank. They're sweet and great dogs, but there's no one in there. They are Doug from the movie *Up*. "Squirrel!" Other dogs have a definite presence, a brightness, an old soul. There is a dog in our neighborhood named Rama, a Bernese Mountain dog who I am certain is an ancient Buddha.

When you looked into Buddy's eyes, you knew that someone was in there, which is why I was so convinced that she would come back in another doggie suit to spend more time with us. She had a special soul. I don't know why she decided to come to earth as a dog. Maybe she really was our guardian angel. I just know that when I looked into that bright, shiny face, all was well with my world.

Buddy brought joy to us and to so many others. Whether it was visiting people at the dog park, on their front porches, or at the market around the corner, people's eyes lit up when they saw her.

The tradition continues. Not too long ago Daisy and I ran into a young man coming out of the store on his way to work. He stopped to pet Daisy, who sat and snuggled into his legs. He looked up, smiling, and said, "Well, she just added a little Sparkle to my day!" So perhaps Daisy is our Little Miss Sparkle.

Buddy put the joy into Christmas for us, too. We don't travel on Christmas, so it can be a quiet morning with two adults opening presents. Since Buddy was our Christmas baby, Christmas became a special time for the three of us. We loved figuring out what presents to get her and how to wrap them so she could help open the packages. Bob had the most fun buying presents for her, while I picked out a few key things for her stocking... a rawhide, a few squeaky balls, maybe some special bones.

Buddy was fascinated by the Christmas tree, and managed to nibble on one of our tin ornaments the first year, despite being under house arrest. We hung that one—embossed with puppy teeth marks—on a low branch every year, even though she never touched it again. I bought thin red and green ribbon so we could tie all the breakable ornaments onto the branches. It looked so pretty, it became a tradition over the years, ensuring that our collection of glass Santas wouldn't get knocked off the tree by an errant, exuberant tail.

Our families played along, with Grandma sending toys or cards with money in them to her grandpuppy Buddy. My sister Melinda sent her a needlepointed pillow one year: "A spoiled dog lives here." It was completely true. We'd clean out the toy bin, donating the spent toys to nearby shelters for other less fortunate pups, and usher in new things to interest her.

Why did we do it? Would she have been content to play with the wrapping paper? Absolutely. But there was such joy in seeing her play with a new toy, nosing her way into the crinkly box, her teeth delicately tearing off an edge. She could tell from the smell which were hers and which were not, and it was only the very last Christmas that she actually unwrapped one of her toys before Christmas morning.

The year Bob got her a radio-controlled mouse was hilarious. It was something I never would have thought to buy, but she lay on the ground and watched it go round and round until she got dizzy.

The balls that lit up and made noise, the huge toys to hump, the covey of squawking waterfowl, the rubber Kongs to hide treats in, the squeaking snakes, the tug toys. All made an appearance under the tree at some point, all were shaken, worried, chased, nosed, and slobbered upon until she flopped on the floor with something in her mouth and fell asleep, while we cleaned up the pile of wrapping paper for another year.

* * *

Our family bought us a lovely gift after she passed, a remembrance kit to plant a gingko tree. It comes with a little engraved tag with the dog's name. We loved that idea, and decided to buy a tree that would embody Buddy Girl's spirit, as gingkos don't thrive in our San Diego climate. I had always wanted a Meyer lemon tree. Meyers are brilliant, sweet yellow lemons, bursting with juice, filled with sunshine. A perfect metaphor for our Buddy Girl.

On Earth Day, three months after Bud left us, we were ready to plant her tree. We chose angel cards again: *Power*, *Patience*, *Freedom*, and *Light*. Notice that we picked *Patience* again. The Universe knows what it's doing.

We chose a spot in the yard with plenty of sunshine that we could see from the kitchen window. Bob dug out the grass and put in the black plastic edging. I had been saving all of the fur I found around the house, the extra biscuits from her last day, and the plastic bag with the last of her dust in it. Once Bob finished the hole we said a little prayer, and I put in her fur, the biscuits, and rinsed out the bag to put the last bit of her essence in there. While Bob planted the tree, I planted Amazon Jewel nasturtium seeds in her honor.

After we finished, I stepped back and looked at the new bed with the tree in the center, and realized that the oval space we had dug out was shaped like a heart.

Meyer lemonade with ginger and lavender —

for people

This sunny, happy drink completely embodies Buddy's lovely spirit: bright, lemony, sweet. Enjoy. Use Meyer lemons if you can find them, as they add a special Buddy-Girl taste to this beverage.

Makes 2-1/2 quarts (*about 2.5 liters*)

2 oz. (*60 g*) ginger root (or one
  good-sized piece)
1/2 C. (*120 ml*) honey or agave syrup
1-1/4 C. (*300 ml*) freshly squeezed Meyer
  lemon juice
organic dried lavender blossoms

   Wash the ginger root and thinly slice. Put it in a saucepan with 1 quart (*1 L*) filtered water and bring just barely to a boil. Cover and turn the heat down to low. Simmer on low for 20 minutes. Turn off and let cool for about 10 minutes.
   Strain into your serving pitcher. Add the honey or agave and stir well to combine.
   Squeeze the lemons.
   Add the lemon juice, stir well, and taste. You may need a little more sweetener. This is purposely strong to stand up to ice.
   Add one spoonful of lavender blossoms to each glass when serving.

Play

Play

One of the great joys in my life right now is watching Daisy play. The pure unfettered joy that she expresses every day is a beautiful thing to behold. It's impossible, even when sad things have happened, to hold sadness in my heart when I'm watching Daisy play.

Puppies playing are simply lovely. They wrestle, jump, growl, and bite in a muscular ballet that teaches them social skills, their place in the world, how to bite gently, and how to get along with strangers. As long as the dogs present themselves with good energy and social cues, a quick butt-sniff is all the information they need to make a new friend and commence wrestling. They sound like they're killing each other, especially when their pearly white teeth Snap! Snap! in the air, but they rarely draw blood. Once they wrap up a round, they will trot off side by side, shaking it off, recharging for the next.

Both Buddy Girl and Daisy have taught us to be more playful. We're more likely to stop working, take a break, and sit on the grass. More likely to go for a walk and romp around, or leap over a short wall once we see that Daisy loves to jump. This is great for both of us, as it's easy to get wrapped up in work and just want to veg out in front of the TV or computer.

We are more likely to be playful with each other, and other people, because we have a dog. It keeps my play skills up to date, so if kids show up at our house or a gathering, I can jump in and play with them without feeling like I've forgotten how.

* * *

Of the two of us, Bob has always been more of the playmate, while I've been the trainer. Watching his unique style of play has always made me smile.

This shy, serious guy was just hilarious with Buddy when they were alone. He would talk to her in funny voices, especially when I wasn't in the room. She would crawl up on his lap with her squeaky ball, and he would bring it to life, making it breathe in her ear. He would animate one of her fuzzy toys, making the arms and legs move while it talked in a high, squeaky voice, which fascinated her no end.

He would cut holes in an empty water bottle, fill it with kibble, and watch her figure out how to get it out. He was the peanut butter man, filling her Kong endlessly, giving her a treat and a challenge. And he was her cookie provider. It didn't take Buddy long to figure out that Bob was the soft touch. She would sit midway between him at the kitchen table and the cookie jar on the counter, and her eyes would go back and forth. Bob. Cookies. Bob. Cookies. Ping. Pong. And then Bob would be up, doing her bidding, opening the jar and feeding her again.

My heart jumped the first time I heard Bob talking to Daisy in his play voice, because I knew then that we were all going to be okay.

Rosemary-olive oil crackers—*for rewarding good dogs,*

or great people

Makes 60-80 small crackers

I used a fancy cookie cutter to show these off for the photo, but scoring with a pizza wheel is easiest. You want them as thin as possible to create a crispy cracker. Some dogs don't like rosemary, so adjust the amount if needed. Skip the salt altogether if making for dogs.

4 T. (*20 g*) flax seeds plus 1/2 C. (*125 ml*) filtered water

1 T. (*5 g*) fresh rosemary (omit or halve for dogs)

1 C. (*120 g*) ground almonds (almond meal or almond flour)

2 C. (*270 g*) sorghum flour

1/4 C. (*60 ml*) olive oil

1/4 C. (*60 ml*) non-dairy milk

1/4 C. (60 ml) filtered water

1 T. (*4 g*) nutritional yeast

1 T. (*18 g*) fine sea salt, divided (omit for dogs)

1 t. (*2 g*) baking soda

These tasty, crispy crackers are another fun dog treat to make that's healthy, wheat-free, and easy. I am sensitive to gluten, as are some dogs, so all my recipes are gluten-free. You can share these treats with your dog in small quantities (any high-fat food can be problematic for dogs).

Cut two pieces of parchment paper the size of two large baking sheets.

Preheat the oven to 425F/*220C/gas mark 6.5*.

Grind the flax seeds in the blender into a fine meal. Put into your mixing bowl with the first 1/2 C. of water to thicken.

Wash and dry the rosemary, then pull all the needles off the sprigs. Finely chop the needles.

Add all the ingredients to your mixing bowl, and blend by hand or with a stand mixer until you have a smooth, sticky dough. If making for people, reserve half the salt to sprinkle on top.

Plop half of the dough on one piece of parchment paper and top with a piece of plastic wrap. Smoosh the dough into a rough circle by hand, then use a rolling pin to roll it out as thin as you can get it. Score the dough into small squares with a pizza cutter (for dogs or people) or use cookie cutters if desired (for people).

Move the whole thing to the baking sheet and repeat with the other half of the dough. If making for people, sprinkle with the rest of the salt.

Bake 12–15 minutes until golden brown and very crispy.

Transfer the parchment paper to wire cooling racks. Store the crackers in an airtight container when completely cool.

Begin Again

Begin Again

Every year I get together with my girlfriends to do vision boards. We've been doing them annually for the last six years and I always look forward to it. Buddy had just died when we were scheduled to meet, so I spent far less time than usual planning my board and searching for photos and words this year.

When I saw the phrase—Begin Again—I knew without a doubt that it was going to be my theme for 2012. I was in my 50th year, starting a new decade, which was exciting. I had been telling people all year that I just turned 50 and I felt like my life was just beginning.

I knew that we had a puppy to look forward to, which would be fun down the road. While we could never replace Buddy Girl, I trusted that we would find another amazing dog to join our family.

What's fascinating about the vision board process is that you never really know how they're going to come true, or what additional meanings are going to emerge from them. Last year's board was called "full circle." There was a spiral staircase in it, and the words "What goes around comes around."

Not only did I see a spiral staircase exactly like that one on our trip to France last year, but so many skills I learned 30 years ago have come around again. I am styling food again, taking photographs again, working in nutrition again.

And I had no idea last January when I made that board that we would come full circle with Bud within a year. While I can't say I would have chosen to "begin again" with Bud, I know that fully embracing it is my path for this year.

...

Four months after Bud passed, we started looking at puppies, visiting two litters (in one backyard) about two hours away from San Diego. We didn't have a good feeling about the breeder or the puppies, and headed home. Bob said, "I think it should feel downstream. Driving two hours feels upstream."

The next Saturday, we saw another litter, with only one girl left. That puppy just didn't seem right to us... she was on the outskirts of the litter, didn't seem to interact well with her litter mates, didn't seem as coordinated, and didn't respond to us at all. While we felt better about the people, and might have chosen a puppy from the litter if we had had more to choose from, this clearly wasn't our dog.

It might take longer than I'd hoped to find our next dog. With Bud it had seemed so easy, I just assumed this time would be, too. I was also shocked at the prices... some puppies cost as much as a decent used car.

As usual, Bob was the voice of reason. "Don't get hung up on when. Don't worry about the price. It will feel downstream. The right dog will come to us." When we got home, it suddenly occurred to me to set up a Google news alert: "golden retriever" + "san diego" + puppies. Two hours later, the email popped up. The first ad was a not-great picture of five puppies who looked just like Buddy behind a chain-link fence. Just about 8 weeks old. Reasonable price. A San Diego area code. The ad had been posted on Tuesday. "Yes, we have two girls and two boys available. Yes, you can come tomorrow. We're in Jamul." Jamul is an hour's drive into East San Diego County, coincidentally where I was supposed to get my very first Buddy, the puppy that fell through.

This breeder was completely different from the other three. Breeding for twenty years. Show dogs and working dogs. Almost never has to advertise, since she has clients coming back time after time. Runs a board-and-care facility. She was located in a gorgeous, quiet, backcountry area, on a road so lovely that I stopped to take pictures, feeling like we were on vacation.

We pulled up, and a pack of dogs came to the gate to greet us, but didn't bark much. Donna came to the gate, and told us to wait while she put the dogs away. They followed her direction perfectly, all heading into the back on command. Everything was tidy. Her manner and the relatively calm energy amongst the pack was a Very Good Sign.

Donna took us in to see the puppies, and gave us each a girl. Now, as mentioned here repeatedly, nothing in the world is cuter than a Golden retriever puppy. Your heart melts to pudding. But after seeing three litters, we were less susceptible, more able to be objective. The parents were mellow, with great spirits and lovely energy. The energy at the ranch was calm. The puppies were calm, with great color. Both girls looked a ton like Buddy at eight weeks.

The one I held first was a bit smaller, blonder, and feistier, just like Bud. Bob was holding the other girl, who was just a sweetheart. You could hold her up or on her back, and she was relaxed, totally chilled out. Very cuddly. Very sweet.

We had talked the night before about what we were looking for. As my grieving eased, I realized it wasn't reasonable to look for Buddy in the new dog. It wasn't likely she would reincarnate and return to us, it wasn't fair to the new dog, and I was bound to be disappointed. Instead I was looking for a dog with a nice, calm personality who we felt a connection with, and who had that spark inside, not one that seemed blank.

As we watched the puppies, held the puppies, it was clear that one of them was right for us. In the end we chose the one less like Bud, so that she could be her own girl, and teach us her own lessons.

Daisy cupcakes—*for people*

Bright sunshiny, happy: the ideal treat to celebrate our little Daisy. When I finally have ripe Meyer lemons from Buddy's tree, this dessert will be a perfect tribute to both our girls.

Makes 24

1 C. (*135 g*) sorghum flour
1 C. (*120 g*) oat flour
1 C. (*160 g*) brown rice flour
1/4 C. (*25 g*) coconut flour
1 T. (*5 g*) baking powder
1 t. (*2 g*) xanthan gum
1 t. (*2 g*) salt
1/2 t. (*1 g*) baking soda
3 T. (*15 g*) flax seeds
6 T. (*90 ml*) filtered water
1 C. (*250 ml*) agave syrup
1 C. (*250 g*) unsweetened applesauce
1/4 C. (*60 ml*) coconut oil
2 T. (*20 ml*) vanilla
zest from 2 lemons
1 C. (*250 ml*) lemon-flavored fizzy mineral water

Preheat oven to 325F/165C/gas mark 3. Line two muffin tins with paper cupcake liners.

Sift and measure the flours into a large bowl. Whisk or sift all the dry ingredients together (the sorghum flour through the baking soda).

Put the flax seeds in a dry blender and grind them until they look like coarse flour. Add the ground flax seeds to the filtered water in a large mixing bowl (the bowl for a stand mixer if you have one) and let it stand five minutes.

Add the agave syrup, applesauce, coconut oil, vanilla, and lemon zest to the mixer bowl and blend until fluffy. You want to add as much air as possible to help create a tender, fluffy cake. With the mixer running on medium, add in the flour mixture a bit at a time until it is thoroughly mixed. Add in the mineral water and mix just until you have a smooth, pourable cake batter.

Using a measuring cup or ice cream scoop, fill the cups no more than 2/3 full.

Bake for 11 minutes. Turn the pans 180 degrees so they bake evenly. Bake another 8 minutes, or until the tops crack a little and a toothpick inserted into the center comes out clean.

Remove from the oven and set on wire racks to cool. When the pans are cool to the touch, remove the cupcakes and set on the wire racks to finish cooling completely.

Vanilla frosting

Makes enough to frost 24 cupcakes
3/4 C. (*180 ml*) unsweetened soy milk
3/4 C. (*275 g*) dry soy or rice milk powder
2/3 C. (*160 ml*) coconut oil
1/4 C. (*60 ml*) light agave syrup
1 T. (*15 ml*) vanilla
1 T. (*15 ml*) lemon juice

1/2 C. (*100 g*) granulated organic sugar, sucanat, or coconut sugar
Up to 1 large spoonful turmeric
1 package shaved or large flake coconut
48 mint leaves
4–6 lemons

Put the granulated sugar in a dry blender, tightly close the lid, and blend on high until it's powdered sugar. Set it aside in a bowl.

Melt the coconut oil by heating water in a microwave-safe bowl and setting the jar in the warm water about 3/4 up the side. Measure it, and set aside.

Add the soy milk, milk powder, agave syrup, vanilla, and lemon juice to the blender. Start on low, then turn it up to high. Leaving the blender running, stream in the coconut oil until you have a thick, creamy consistency.

Scrape out the frosting into a medium-sized bowl. Slowly stir in the powdered sugar until you get a fairly thick frosting consistency. Stir in the turmeric a little at a time until you get the yellow color you want. (Don't worry; it doesn't make it taste like curry.) The frosting will thicken if chilled.

• • •

To decorate:

Spread each cooled cupcake with frosting.

Form the daisy petals from long pieces of coconut, adding them in a circle, with the curves all facing the same direction.

Use an apple corer to cut a perfect circle of lemon rind, then carefully slice off just the yellow rind with a sharp paring knife.

Add the lemon rind circle to the center of the daisy.

Just before serving, add two mint leaves. (Remove the mint leaves before storing.)

Notes: To get a whiter frosting/topping, you need to use lighter ingredients. Rice milk powder is lighter in color than soy milk powder. Organic granulated sugar is lighter than coconut sugar. Choose light amber agave syrup.

What I've learned from Buddy Girl and Daisy May

When you smile at the world, the world smiles back.

Everyone is your friend. Even if someone bites you... it's just about them, it's not about you.

Rolling around in the grass is fun. So is digging in a sand pit. So is napping in the shade.

There are amazing things to see and smell if you just slow down.

If you do new things, you meet great people. Those people can become lifelong friends.

Cookies are good.

Dried liver is worth running for.

People who give you cookies are especially good.

Loving unconditionally is the best gift in the whole world.

Thank you, girls.

Buddy Girl   Daisy May

Thanks

First of all, this book is for Buddy Girl, who changed my life in more ways than I can express. For Bob, who I cannot imagine life without, and without whom I may not have become a Golden owner. To my local writing group: Laura Bashar, Kim Burnell, Lisa Dearen, Mimi Holtz, Mary Papoulias-Platis, Liz Schmitt, and Priscilla Willis. Without your generosity, encouragement, and deadlines, I would never have sent *Golden Angels* to an editor, may not have finished it, and definitely would not be taking the leap into print. My editor Maraya Cornell, who helped shape this book, and my designer Tanya Bredehoft, who made it beautiful. I am grateful to my volunteer copy editors Marjorie Schwarzer (who took out all those pesky commas) and Susan Cesen, the Typo Ninja. To my friends in the blogging community—especially my food blogger peeps, the women of Generation Fabulous, Vicki Abelson's Women Who Write, and the APE group on Google +, thank you for all the ways you helped this book get out into the world.

Thanks to my Kickstarter angels: Ellen & David Dolgen, Ann & Thayer Lindner, Patricia McCausland, Joanna Perry-Folino, and Tom Richter.

To all my Kickstarter backers: I am more grateful than you will ever know for your support.

And to all the beautiful dogs who surround us with their joy, love, and sweet presence.

Thank you.

About the author

Stephanie Weaver is an experience consultant, TEDx speaker coach, recipe developer, and food photographer. She finds inspiration and delight as an occasional yogi, urban farmer, and puppy wrangler. She lives in San Diego with her husband Bob and their golden retriever, Daisy.

Her first book, *Creating Great Visitor Experiences: A Guide for Museums, Parks, Zoos, Gardens, and Libraries* is in its 6th printing.

Look for her *Twelve Terrific* recipe collections online.

Find her on the web as her alter ego, The Recipe Renovator, creating ridiculously yummy, gluten-free recipes made from plants.

Contact your local humane society for more pet loss resources and support.

Book Club Discussion Questions

Have you ever created a ritual to mark a significant life event? What did you do and how did it help you?

How did the recipes move the story forward?

Were you surprised at the level of grief the author expressed over losing her dog? Why or why not?

Do you think the author believes in reincarnation? Why or why not? Do you?

The theme of angels runs throughout the book. Do you believe in angels?

The author describes an experience of communicating with Buddy Girl in yoga class. Have you ever had a similar experience?

Is there a particular recipe that you hold dear in your life that ties back to a particular event?

Do you agree with the author's description of the difference between grieving and wallowing?

The message the author received from Buddy Girl in yoga class was, "You can miss me without being sad." What did you think that meant?

What is the first recipe you would make from the book? Why?

What are some of the gifts you have received from a pet?

Do you still think about lost pets? When do they come to mind?

Was there one scene you especially related to? Why?

The author and her husband describe using angel cards for guidance. Did you feel comfortable or uncomfortable with this concept? Have you ever used a similar tool in your life for guidance?

Do you think the book is hopeful?

Book Club

Memories of